A Timeless Perspec

Perceiving and Mar

Information in Our Imprecise World

DATA

AND REALITY

third edition

A Timeless Perspective on Perceiving and Managing Information in Our Imprecise World

DATA
AND REALITY

third edition

WILLIAM KENT

Updated by Steve Hoberman

Technics Publications

Published by:

Technics Publications, LLC
966 Woodmere Drive
Westfield, NJ 07090 U.S.A.
www.technicspub.com

Edited by David Kent and Carol Lehn
Cover design by Mark Brye
Cartoons by Abby Denson, www.abbycomix.com

Original Content from 2nd Edition Copyright © 2012 by David Kent
Commentary from Steve Hoberman Copyright © 2012 by Technics Publications, LLC

ISBN, print ed.   978-1-9355042-1-4

First Printing 2012
Library of Congress Control Number: 2012930842

ATTENTION SCHOOLS AND BUSINESSES: Technics Publications books are available at quantity discounts with bulk purchase for educational, business, or sales promotional use. For information, please email Steve Hoberman, President of Technics Publications, at me@stevehoberman.com.

An excellent, philosophical discussion of the problems inherent in describing the real world. There is nothing really similar to this work. I think that all database researchers should read this document.

Mike Senko, 1978

I expect the book to be one of the most frequently quoted ones for the next few years. It is unique in being an almost exhaustive, condensed rendition of the typical problems encountered. The most striking strong point is its penetration into major database technology headaches.... Many well-chosen examples and the lucid style make it easy to read.

Reiner Durcholz, 1978

Kent has produced a rather remarkable and highly readable short work...the most important things he has to say are philosophical and go right to the heart of the key concepts that must be understood if a system is to be "successful" (whatever that may mean!).... This is a serious book but not a heavy one. Kent writes easily and without hiding behind the semantics of the data base specialists.

Datamation, March 1979

Data and Reality *illustrates extensively the pitfalls of any simplistic attempts to capture reality as data in the sense of today's database systems. The approach taken by the author is one which very logically and carefully delineates the facets of reality being represented in an information system, and also describes the data processing models used in such systems. The linguistic, semantic, and philosophical problems of describing reality are comprehensively examined.... The depth of discussion of these concepts, as they impact information systems, is not likely to be found elsewhere.... [T]he value of this book resides in its critical, probing approach to the difficulties of modeling reality in typical information systems.... [I]t is very well written and should prove both enjoyable and enlightening to a careful reader.*

ACM Computing Reviews, August 1980

Kent attacks the pseudo-exactness of existing data models in a very neat and clear (and often humorous) manner.... This book is for everyone who thinks about or works on data files and who wants to understand the reasons for his disenchantment.

European Journal of Operations Research, November 1981

I am using **Data and Reality** *as research material for my current project. It is on my desk right now.*

Joe Celko, 1998

The book is still quoted quite often and has a message even—or especially—for today's jaded information scientists.

Prof. Dr. Robert Meersman, Vrije Universiteit Brussel, 1998

Your book focuses attention on many issues that are still, embarrassingly, not being dealt with in our formalized information systems. It provides an important reference point not only in identifying these problems, but in pointing out origins and the long-standing practice of simply ignoring them. When I reopened your book...I found lots of issues that seem as fresh as ever.

Roger Burkhart, John Deere, 1998

A small number of computing and information management books are of foundational nature, not oriented towards a particular technology, methodology or tool. **Data and Reality** *is such a book. The concepts and approach described there are as valid now as they were in 1978, and are still often ignored resulting in systems that are not what we want them to be.*

Haim Kilov, Genesis Development Corporation, 1999

Were it not for Bill Kent I might have forgotten that the data represented by that richness was only a representation of reality, and not the reality itself. In a world which reinvents the Perfect Semantic Representation Language to End All Semantic Representation Languages every ten years or so, it is a pleasure to have Bill's calming influence in print in the form of **Data and Reality***.*

Richard Mark Soley, Ph.D., CEO, Object Management Group, 1999

I served on the original ANSI X3H2 Database Standards Committee with Bill Kent—these were the pioneer days of RDBMS. The relational model was still new, and the academics were playing with relational algebra as a high level abstraction. We had set theory, relations. We had semiotics, formal languages and other conceptual tools. And they never got together! How long did we have wheels? How long did we have suitcases? So why did it take so long to put wheels on suitcases? **Data and Reality** *was the first book to look at data qua data by putting all of the tools in one place. We were still learning and Bill was ahead of the rest of us. My work with designing data encoding schemes was inspired by this book. Looking at the third edition with Steve's commentaries, I am reminded just how important this book was and still is. I tell people this is like reading a copy of Sun Tsu's* **Art of War** *with good updated commentaries.*

Joe Celko, Author of eight books on SQL, 2012

I knew Bill Kent before he was Bill Kent—he always had these searching thoughts, profound questions. Talking with Bill Kent made you aware that you were talking with someone that had thought longer and more deeply than you. He might have written **Data and Reality** *in 1978, but it is still years ahead of its time! I think Bill is the first one, certainly the first one I ever knew, that understood that meaning (semantics) is expressed in the structural characteristics of the components (the actual "things") of interest. In the automated systems domain, what* **is** *well understood by IT is "GARBAGE IN, GARBAGE OUT." If data meaning is not precisely expressed in the structure of a data model, I am going to guarantee there is a lot of garbage spewing out of the Enterprises' systems! Everybody, (IT and non-IT) ought to read Bill's book and get their garbage data cleaned up—they owe it to their neighbors!*

John Zachman, 2012

Contents

A Note by Chris Date on the Republication of *Data and Reality*

By Chris Date in 2012

I first read this book in draft form in the mid-1970s, and I enjoyed it immensely. Bill was a good friend of mine; we had many interests in common, including not least a deep and abiding love of the desert. Although we didn't always see eye to eye technically, our debates on technical issues were never acrimonious, and often enlightening to me. Of course, the world has moved on since then; I've learned a lot myself in the intervening years, and I'm quite sure there are aspects of Bill's book that I would disagree with now more than I did then! (His characterization of the relational model is certainly a case in point.) But this is quibbling. Here's a lightly edited version of what I wrote myself by way of annotation on his book when I referenced it some years later in a book of my own:

> *[Bill's book is a] stimulating and thought-provoking discussion of the nature of information.... "This book projects a philosophy that life and reality are at bottom amorphous, disordered, contradictory, inconsistent, non-rational, and nonobjective" (excerpt from the final chapter). The book can be regarded in large part as a compendium of real-world problems that (it is suggested) existing database formalisms have difficulty in dealing with. Recommended.*

I still stand by these remarks today. (Though I have to say that the reference to "a compendium of real-world problems" does remind me—I don't think Bill would mind me saying this—that I always thought of Bill as being, philosophically, at one with the apocryphal trainee officer of whom an exasperated instructor wrote in his final report: "This man can be relied upon to find the set of circumstances in which any given plan can be guaranteed not to work.")

In all seriousness, though, I'm very glad to see Bill's book being given a new lease on life in this way. I hope it wins him many new fans. For me, it brings Bill very strongly back to mind, and in my imagination I can see his face again and hear once again his gruff voice saying "But what about...." I wish the book every success.

Foreword to the New Edition of *Data and Reality*

By Graeme Simsion in 2012

With a single word, *Data and Reality* lays down a challenge to data modeling practitioners, teachers, and researchers.

The word is *arbitrary*, which Merriam-Webster defines as "...based on or determined by individual preference or convenience...." William Kent uses the word throughout the book—and particularly in the first chapter—to characterize some of the most important decisions that data modelers make.

The boundaries of an entity are arbitrary, our selection of entity types is arbitrary, the distinction between entities, attributes, and relationships is arbitrary. In a similar vein, he uses variants of the word *ambiguous* some fifty times, pointing out important and often fundamental problems with the goals, language, and process of data modeling.

Kent was writing in 1978, when data modeling was a new discipline. His achievement at the time was to identify the areas in which we needed to develop theory and experience so that critical data modeling decisions could be rooted in something more than "individual preference."

In the years since, hundreds of books and papers have been published on data modeling, and practitioners have accumulated a wealth of experience. So we should be well down the track towards replacing arbitrariness with soundly-based rules and guidelines. Unfortunately, this is not the case, at least not in the areas that *Data and Reality* focuses on. Nor have Kent's concerns been further elaborated, or, for that matter, refuted.

Instead, like the drunk looking for his lost keys under the streetlamp because "the light is better here," we have pursued other, less fundamental, aspects of data modeling, in particular the design and evaluation of modeling formalisms (within a sadly unimaginative range of variants). The only significant exception is the exploration of the binary alternative to the entity-relationship-attribute paradigm by Nijssen, Halpin, and others, which Kent foreshadows in Chapters 4 and 5. But, again, this work has led mainly to proposals for new formalisms. Similarly, research that seeks to apply ontology to data modeling has focused on comparing formalisms, rather than shedding light on the deeper questions that Kent raises.

The arbitrariness that Kent identifies lies in the earliest—and, I would argue, the most critical—stage of data modeling, when complex real-world structures are mapped onto the simple constructs supported by the modeling language. My own research with data modeling practitioners in 2002-2006 showed considerable evidence of arbitrary decisions, resulting in radically different models for the same situation—with little basis for choosing one over the others. Worse, many modelers seemed unaware of the arbitrariness of their models, and hence were inclined to see alternative models as being wrong, rather than the result of different arbitrary decisions. Thought leaders were divided about the contribution of individual preference: some saw modeling as deterministic, others as highly creative.

So, more than three decades on from *Data and Reality*, data modelers still do not have a clear agreement on the nature of the task, on what guidelines to apply in selecting entities, attributes, and relationships, and why one workable model should be preferred over another.

Perhaps we have avoided these issues because they lead to the difficult questions of identity, semantics, and categorization, which are traditionally the territory of philosophers rather than information technology practitioners and researchers. But we will not find our keys if we are not prepared to move from under the streetlamp.

The practitioner or researcher who is not equipped or inclined to tackle these problems at least needs to be aware of them, in order to understand the challenges of their work and the limitations of the techniques they are using. Researchers need to understand, deeply, the shortcomings of laboratory tasks that require the participant to develop a single correct "gold standard" model for a situation, and of formalisms and quality metrics that assume a common perception and categorization of the real-world domain. Practitioners need to recognize where they are making arbitrary decisions that might well be different from those made by other modelers.

While such fundamental issues remain unrecognized and unanswered, *Data and Reality*, with its lucid and compelling elucidation of the questions, needs to remain in print. I read the book as a database administrator in 1980, as a researcher in 2002, and just recently as the manuscript for the present edition. On each occasion, I found something more, and on each occasion I considered it the most important book I had read on data modeling. It has been on my recommended reading list forever. The first chapter, in particular, should be mandatory reading for anyone involved in data modeling.

In publishing this new edition, Steve Hoberman has not only ensured that one of the key books in the data modeling canon remains in print, but has added his own comments and up-to-date examples, which are likely to be helpful to those who have come to data modeling more recently. Don't do any more data modeling work until you've read it.

About Graeme

Graeme Simsion is an information systems consultant, educator and researcher with a longstanding interest in data modeling. He is the author of *Data Modeling Essentials*, which is now entering its fourth edition, and of numerous academic and practitioner papers. His Ph.D. thesis, published as *Data Modeling Theory and Practice*, reported on the attitudes and practices of almost five hundred data modeling practitioners. He currently focuses on teaching consulting skills and pursuing his second career as a screenwriter.

Preface to the Third Edition

By Steve Hoberman in 2012

Travel back with me to the year 1978.

The New York Yankees win the World Series, Montreal takes the Stanley Cup, Borg is the Wimbledon champion, and Argentina wins the World Cup. *Annie Hall* wins the Oscar for Best Picture, *You Light Up My Life* wins the Oscar for best song, and the record of the year is *Hotel California* by The Eagles. We can reminisce on fashion (and yes, I did own a pair of bell bottoms) and politics (Peanuts, anybody?), but instead, let's look at the world of technology in 1978.

1978 was a monumental year for technology. Sony introduced the world's first portable stereo, the Sony Walkman®. Your "coolness factor" in school was directly proportional to whether you had an original Walkman or one of the many cheap knockoffs. Also in 1978, Illinois Bell Company introduced the first cellular mobile phone system. Do you remember those "portable" large shoulder-bag mobile phones first came in? This same year, the first computer bulletin board system (BBS) was created. (I remember buying a used refrigerator off a BBS.) Also monumental this year, Space Invaders made its debut and the craze for video games began.

In addition to the start of the age for portable music, cell phones, online commerce, and video games, 1978 was also a banner year for data management. The relational model had a big win over the hierarchical and network models: Oracle Version 1 was announced in 1978, written in assembly language and running on a whopping 128K of memory. Version 2 (in 1980) became the first commercially available relational database to use SQL. And also in 1978, William Kent wrote *Data and Reality*.

I won't get into how much a dozen eggs cost in 1978 or a newly constructed home, but the point is important seeds were planted in 1978, and these seeds have grown into massive trees in the forms of the awesome technology we have today. From the Walkman to the iPod®, from cell phones weighing 20 pounds to those the size of credit cards, from bulletin board systems to 100,000 virtual stores, including Amazon and eBay, from one relational database option to many options—even columnar, XML, and NOSQL databases—there is no doubt we have made amazing leaps in technology since 1978.

Therefore, you would expect anything technology-related from 1978 to be prehistoric, useless, and perhaps even laughable today. Not so with *Data and Reality*.

What strongly attracted me to the book *Data and Reality* was the large amount of material that is still directly relevant to us in data management today. It is a special book—not a "how to do" book on data management (such as how to normalize attributes or create a database), but a "how to think" book on data management. *Data and Reality* weaves the disciplines of psychology and philosophy gracefully with data management. Issues relative to how we perceived and managed information in 1978 were no different from how we think of information today. This book is technology-independent, and therefore timeless in its messages, regardless of whether we are a 1970s data processing expert or a modern day data analyst, data modeler, database administrator, or data architect.

This concept of applying human nature to a discipline and showing the "mind game" under the discipline can define a field of study. In fact, I take a break from typing this paragraph and walk to my bookshelf, where I see "mind game" books in other disciplines, all, interestingly, written in the 1970s, and still useful texts today:

- Gerald Weinberg wrote *The Psychology of Computer Programming* in 1971, and its content is still very useful today. All points dealing with the human elements of software creation, such as ego and humility, are just as valid today as they were when this book was written.
- W. Timothy Gallwey wrote *The Inner Game of Tennis* in 1974; you can still learn amazing concentration and mental game techniques for tennis today. The way we think in terms of Self 1 (the "teller") and Self 2 (the "doer") is something I will teach my daughters as they continue to master this game. Your success on the court is directly related to what is going on in your mind.
- Frederick Brooks wrote *The Mythical Man-Month* on software engineering back in 1974. Many of the key messages, such as the value of project team communication, can be applied in the project team trenches today, regardless of whether traditional software waterfall or agile methodologies are being deployed.

This book is written for anyone who needs to understand the data mind game. If you are responsible for eliciting, analyzing, modeling, designing, developing, supporting, governing, or managing applications that need or modify data, you need to know the data mind game and should read this book.

This book will make you think! This starts right in Kent's preface in the next section where Kent relates his own life to the concepts of existence, identity, attributes, relationships, behavior, and modeling. To prepare you for his discussion of these terms,

I will relate each of these six terms to data modeling using an account example, and also introduce here how to read a data model.

Imagine that you go into a bank and open an account. If you were not a prior customer of the bank, you are now a customer of the bank after opening the account.

Kent first refers to "existence." Do you as a customer exist in the bank's world if you had no accounts? Does your account exist if you don't exist? Kent next uses the term "identity." Does the bank need to know your account information to identify you? That is, if your name is Bob Jones, and there are two Bob Joneses in this particular bank, does your account information distinguish you from this other Bob Jones? Also does the bank need to know information about you to identify your account?

Kent continues with the term "attributes." What is important to capture about you as a customer? About your account? It could be your name, birthday, and address. It could be your account number and the minimum monthly balance before you are charged fees. Kent then introduces "relationships." Can you own more than one account? Can the account you just opened be owned by only you or jointly with someone else, such as a spouse? "Behavior" is the next term. What do you do now that you are a customer? What does your account do? Your account might now, for example, act as a medium for depositing and withdrawing funds. With regard to Kent's last term of "modeling," how do I take the answers to all of the questions in the above paragraph and represent them precisely and in an easily digestible format so that I now have an effective communication tool?

For example, if you, as a Customer, can exist without owning any Accounts and also can own one or more Accounts, and an Account can exist only if it is related to a single Customer, then this would be the resulting data model:

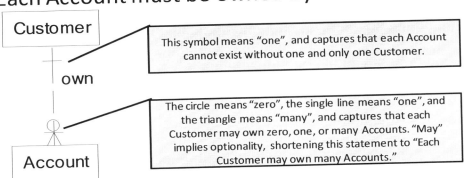

Each Customer may own one or many Accounts.
Each Account must be owned by one Customer.

Customer

own

Account

This symbol means "one", and captures that each Account cannot exist without one and only one Customer.

The circle means "zero", the single line means "one", and the triangle means "many", and captures that each Customer may own zero, one, or many Accounts. "May" implies optionality, shortening this statement to "Each Customer may own many Accounts."

If however, a Customer cannot exist without owning at least one Account, then this would be the resulting data model:

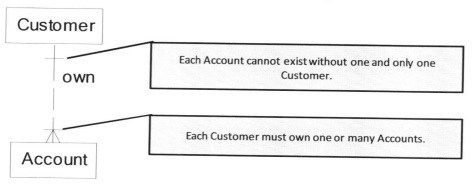

Each Customer must own one or many Accounts.
Each Account must be owned by one Customer.

Customer

own

Each Account cannot exist without one and only one Customer.

Each Customer must own one or many Accounts.

Account

If a Customer can exist without owning any Accounts and can also own more than one Account, and an Account can exist without being owned by a single Customer and can be owned by at most one Customer, then this would be the resulting data model:

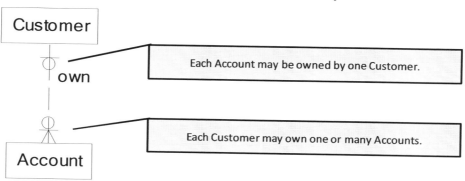

Each Customer may own one or many Accounts.
Each Account may be owned by one Customer.

Customer

own

Each Account may be owned by one Customer.

Each Customer may own one or many Accounts.

Account

This is the third edition of *Data and Reality*, and differs in three main ways from the first and second editions:

1. I have added commentary throughout the chapters. To distinguish it from the original text, my commentary is always indented and in italics and follows the paragraph to which it is related. There are two reasons for this commentary. The first reason is to bring certain terminology up to date to help you relate to Kent's very important messages. The second reason is to expand on Kent's messages with my own messages and experiences. The overall goal of my commentary is to make sure you get as much as you can from this book.

2. I have added "Steve's Takeaways" to the end of each chapter. These are the most important messages that I learned from each chapter. You can use these messages to reinforce what you received from the chapter, or as the start of a brainstorming exercise with colleagues to come up with your own key messages from each chapter.

3. I removed several sections of the book that are less relevant today than in 1978, along with updating terms and references, and adding footnotes where appropriate.

I encourage you to come up with your own insights after reading this text. In fact, please share your insights with me. I'm interested. You can email me at me@stevehoberman.com, use the Twitter hashtag #DataAndReality, or follow me @DataModlRockStar.

Enjoy, and learn!

About Steve

Steve is currently a data modeling consultant and instructor. He taught his first data modeling class in 1992 and has educated more than 10,000 people about data modeling and business intelligence techniques since then. Steve balances the formality and precision of data modeling with the realities of building software systems with severe time, budget, and people constraints. In his consulting and teaching, he focuses on templates, tools, and guidelines to reap the benefits of data modeling with minimal investment. Steve is the author of five books on data modeling, the founder of the Design Challenges group, and inventor of the Data Model Scorecard®.

Preface to the Second Edition

By William Kent in 2000

Despite critical acclaim, outside of a small circle of enthusiastic readers this book has been a sleeper for over twenty years. Publishers have recently offered to market and distribute it with more vigor if I would provide a new revised edition, but I've resisted. Laziness might be seen as the excuse, but I'm beginning to realize there's a better reason.

A new revised edition would miss the point of the book. Many texts and reference works are available to keep you on the leading edge of data processing technology. That's not what this book is about. This book addresses timeless questions about how we as human beings perceive and process information about the world we operate in, and how we struggle to impose that view on our data processing machines. The concerns at this level are the same, whether we use hierarchical[1], relational, or object-oriented[2] information structures; whether we process data via punched-card machines or interactive graphic interfaces[3]; whether we correspond by paper mail or e-mail; whether we shop from paper-based catalogs or the web. No matter what the technology, these underlying issues have to be understood. Failure to address these issues imperils the success of your application, regardless of the tools you are using.

That's not to say the technical matrix of the book is obsolete or antiquated. The data record is still a fundamental component of the way we organize computer information. Sections of the book exploring new models, including behavioral elements, are precursors of object orientation.

The scope of the book extends beyond computer technology. The questions aren't so much about how we process data as about how we perceive reality, about the constructs and tactics we use to cope with complexity, ambiguity, incomplete information, mismatched viewpoints, and conflicting objectives.

---

[1] Such as an XML style sheet

[2] Such as a Unified Modeling Language (UML) use case or class diagram

[3] Such as a form on a web page

You can read the book for those reasons or for other reasons, as well. A few years back, almost twenty years after the book was published, I began to notice that the book is also about something else, something far more personal. The scope of the book doesn't only extend beyond computer data processing into the realm of how we perceive the world. It also extends into our inner domain. I've come to recognize that it touches on issues in my own inner life that I, like most of us to some degree or other, have been grappling with for decades.

Consider the key topics: existence, identity, attributes, relationships, behavior, and modeling.

- **Existence:** Is *cogito ergo sum* sufficient? To what extent am I really present and engaged in the process of life around me? How real are the physical things I experience? To what extent do I exist in some spiritual realm independent of the physical context?

- **Identity:** The old "Who am I?" bit. What is the true nature of the kind of person I am? What sorts of needs, goals, and outlooks define who I really am?

- **Attributes:** What kind of person am I? What are my values, my assets, my limitations?

- **Relationships:** This is the core of it all. What is the quality of my interaction with parents, lovers, spouses, children, siblings, friends, colleagues, and other acquaintances? What are my connections with things material, social, spiritual, and otherwise? What are my needs here? What are the issues and problems? How can they be improved?

- **Behavior:** What should I plan to do in various situations? How? What might be the consequences, both intended and otherwise? What contingencies need to be anticipated?

- **Modeling:** How accurate and useful are the constructs I use to explain all these things? How effective are these kinds of explanations in helping me change what needs to be changed?

This book certainly shouldn't be classified in the social sciences, but it is remarkable to observe how technology issues can resonate as metaphors for our inner lives. This perspective seems to explain why I've engaged so intimately with these ideas, why I've argued so passionately about them at standards committee meetings and in the hallways at conferences.

Kent isn't alone here. The data management industry is full of passionate people. When I attend a data management conference, for example, I see the same people continuously striving (and sometimes fighting!) year after year to improve the data quality and data management within their organizations. We get red in the face when we hear stories of how Wild West developers completely disregard data modeling and applaud when we hear a success story where the project was delivered on time and under budget and yes, the team did pretty good data modeling work as well!

Another story to illustrate data management passion. Years ago I was in a meeting with fellow data modelers reviewing one of my models and a modeler in the room so passionately argued a point on the model, that she literary got out of her seat and stood up on the table to argue her position—now that's passion for our field!

I repeat the invitation, made in the book's original preface, to discover for yourself what you might think the book is about. It just might be about you. But if that's too much pop psychology for your comfort, if that's too invasive of your personal space, then just read it for its insights into data processing and reality.

By William Kent in 1978

A message to mapmakers: Highways are not painted red, rivers don't have county lines running down the middle, and you can't see contour lines on a mountain.

> *This opening sentence summarizes why maps are amazing. We can read a map and know what it is representing even though the symbols and text on the map look nothing like what they represent. A map is a set of symbols and text used for explaining something complex with a visually simple representation.*

> *A map simplifies a complex geographic landscape in the same way that a data model simplifies a complex information landscape. (For a more thorough explanation of data modeling, see my book **Data Modeling Made Simple 2nd Edition**, published by Technics Publications in 2009.) A line represents a motorway on a map of France. A rectangle containing the word "Customer" on a data model represents the concept of a real Customer such as Bob, IBM, or Walmart. A data model is a set of symbols and text which precisely explains a*

subset of real information to improve communication within the organization and thereby lead to a more flexible and stable application environment.

Perhaps the most common form of data model we work with on a daily basis is the spreadsheet. A spreadsheet is a representation of a paper worksheet, containing a grid defined by rows and columns, where each cell in the grid can contain text or numbers. The columns often contain different types of information. Unlike a spreadsheet, however, the data model that is the focus of this book:

- *Contains only types. Data models don't usually display actual values such as "Bob" and "Saturday." Data models display concepts or types. So, a data model would display the entity type Customer, instead of showing the actual value "Bob" and the attribute Day of Week instead of the actual value "Saturday."*

- *Contains interactions. Data models capture how concepts interact with each other. For example, a Customer can own one or many Accounts, and an Account must be owned by one and only one Customer.*

- *Provides a concise communication medium. A single sheet of paper containing a data model communicates much more than a single piece of paper containing a spreadsheet. Data models display types, not actual values, and they use simple yet powerful symbols to communicate interactions. We can capture all of the types and interactions within the customer account area in a much more concise format using a data model rather than in a spreadsheet.*

For some time now my work has concerned the representation of information in computers. The work has involved such things as file organizations, indexes, hierarchical structures, network structures, relational models, and so on. After a while it dawned on me that these are all just maps, being poor artificial approximations of some real underlying terrain.

These structures give us useful ways to deal with information, but they don't always fit naturally, and sometimes not at all. Like different kinds of maps, each kind of structure has its strengths and weaknesses, serving different purposes, and appealing to different people in different situations. Data structures are artificial formalisms. They differ from information in the same sense that grammars don't describe the language we really use, and formal logical systems don't describe the way we think. "The map is not the territory" [Hayakawa].

What is the territory really like? How can I describe it to you? Any description I give you is just another map. But we do need some language (and I mean natural language) in order to discuss this subject, and to articulate concepts. Such constructs as "entities," "categories," "names," "relationships," and "attributes" seem to be useful. They give us at least one way to organize our perceptions and discussions of information. In a sense, such terms represent the basis of my "data structure," or "model," for perceiving real information. Later chapters discuss these constructs and their central characteristics— especially the difficulties involved in trying to define or apply them precisely.

Along the way, we implicitly suggest a hypothesis (by sheer weight of examples, rather than any kind of proof—such a hypothesis is beyond proof): There is probably no adequate formal modeling system. Information in its "real" essence is probably too amorphous, too ambiguous, too subjective, too slippery and elusive, to ever be pinned down precisely by the objective and deterministic processes embodied in a computer. (At least in the conventional uses of computers as we see them today; future developments in artificial intelligence may endow these machines with more of our capacity to cope.) This follows a path pointed out by Zemanek, connecting data processing with certain philosophical observations about the real world, especially the aspects of human judgment on which semantics ultimately depend ([Zemanek 72]).

In spite of such difficulties (and because I see no alternative), we also begin to explore the extent and manner in which such constructs can be and have been incorporated into various data models. We are looking at real information, as it occurs in the interactions among people, but always with a view toward modeling that information in a computer-based system.

The questions are these: What is a useful way to perceive information for that purpose? What constructs are useful for organizing the way we think about information? Might those same constructs be employed in a computer based model of the information? How successfully are they reflected in current modeling systems? How badly oversimplified is the view of information in currently used data models? Are there limits to the effectiveness of any system of constructs for modeling information?

In spite of my conjecture about the inherent limits of formal modeling, we do need models in order to go about our business of processing information. Keep in mind that I am not talking about "information" in a very broad sense. I am not talking about very ambitious information systems. We are not in the domain of artificial intelligence, where the effort is to match the intellectual capabilities of the human mind (reasoning, inference, value judgments, etc.). We are not even trying to process prose text; we are not attempting to understand natural language, analyze grammar, or retrieve information from documents. We are primarily concerned with that kind of information which is managed in most current files and databases. We are looking at information that occurs in large quantities, is permanently maintained, and has some simplistic structure and format to it. Examples include personnel files, bank records, and inventory records.

> *Although we are not in the domain of artificial intelligence, we are in the domain of "business intelligence." Business intelligence is the process of turning data into information so business professionals can make more intelligent business decisions. In addition to traditional structured sources, today information **can** involve understanding natural languages and retrieving information from documents; for example, in searching blog postings and discussion groups for feedback on a certain product.*

Even this modest bit of territory offers ample opportunity for misunderstanding the semantics of the information being represented.

Within these bounds, we focus on describing the information content of some system. The system involved might be one or more files, a database, a system catalog, a data dictionary, or perhaps something else. We are limiting ourselves to the information content of such systems, excluding such concerns as:

- Real implementations, representation techniques, performance.
- Manipulation and use of the data.
- Work flow, transactions, scheduling, message handling.
- Integrity, recovery, security.

> *Data models do present a filtered and incomplete representation of a business area. A data model is a set of symbols and text for representing information in an easy-to-understand way. An easy-to-understand visual, however, focuses only on information and ignores other useful characteristics of the existing or proposed system, such as the business process. For example, a data model will capture that a customer must own at least one account, but not capture the process of how that customer opened their account.*

A caution to the lay reader in search of a tutorial: This book is not about data processing as it is. As obvious as these concepts may seem, they are not reflected in, or are just dimly understood in, the current state of data processing systems. "We do not, it seems, have a very clear and commonly agreed upon set of notions about data—either what they are, how they should be fed and cared for, or their relation to the design of programming languages and operating systems" [Mealy]. That opening paragraph of a now classic paper, some ten years old, is still distressingly apt today.

> *Mealy wrote this in 1967. Unfortunately and unbelievably, I believe it is still true today!*

There is a wonderful irony at work here. I may be trying to overcome misconceptions which people outside the computer business don't have in the first place. Many readers will find little new in what I say about the nature of our perceptions of reality. Such readers may well react with "So what's new?" To them, my point is that the computing community has largely lost sight of such truisms. Their relevance to the computing disciplines needs to be re-established.

> *There is a "gap" that often exists within the same organization between the information technology department and the rest of the organization. Building on Kent's comments that the computing community (today called the information technology department, or IT department, for short) has "lost sight of such truisms," I believe much of this gap is due to the different view of technology and information. Many business professionals view information technology as an enabler to better understand their business and therefore improve their organization in some way. Many IT departments, however, retain the 1970s view of information technology as a required cost center to protect and buffer business professionals from systems and information. When computers were new, complex, and frightening, this view as a protector worked fine. But today, technology is much more user-friendly and business professionals are much more technology-savvy.*
>
> *I highly recommend the book **fruITion** (IT for information technology) as a good read which explores this business and IT gap. At one point in the novel, the CEO says to the CIO, "Do you know, I've just realized something that I've been wondering about IT for ages? Why nobody really values what you lot do" [Potts 08]. This conversation early in the book is followed by a number of events which eventually make the CIO implement a different operating model so that IT is viewed more as an investment instead of a cost center.*

People in the data processing community have gotten used to viewing things in a highly simplistic way, dictated by the kind of tools they have at their disposal. And this may suggest another wonderful irony. People are awed by the sophistication and complexity of computers, and tend to assume that such things are beyond their comprehension. But that view is entirely backwards! The thing that makes computers so hard to deal with is not their complexity, but their utter simplicity. The first thing that ought to be explained to the general public is that a computer possesses incredibly little ordinary intelligence. The real mystique behind computers is how anybody can manage to get such elaborate behavior out of such a limited set of basic capabilities. Imagine, for example, a person who only understood grammatically perfect sentences, and couldn't make the slightest allowance for colloquialisms, or for the normal way people restart sentences in mid-speech, or for the trivial typographical errors which we correct so automatically that we don't even see them. The first step toward understanding computers is an appreciation of their simplicity, not their complexity.

Another thought, though: I may be going off in the wrong direction by focusing so much concern on computers and computer thinking. Many of the concerns about the semantics of data seem relevant to any record keeping facility, whether computerized or not. I wonder why the problems appear to be aggravated in the environment of a computerized database. Is it sheer magnitude? Perhaps there is just a larger mass of people than before who need to achieve a common understanding of what the data means. Or is it the lost human element? Maybe all those conversations with secretaries and clerks, about where things are and what they mean, are more essential to the system than we've realized. Or is there some other explanation?

Kent raises a very important question here: Why are the issues bigger when a computer system is involved? I think what causes the data issues to become magnified when using systems as opposed to pencil and paper, are three things: systems complexity, role specialization, and tainted thinking.

Systems complexity means that in most organizations, there are multiple applications, with each application having a different purpose. When I worked for the phone company, for example, our company estimated that the subscriber's name and phone number existed in more than 250 distinct places! Departments and functional areas build their own applications, and create and recreate the same data, often with different constraints and definitions, causing an incredible amount of complexity at an organizational level. This systems complexity becomes magnified when one organization purchases another organization, which is happening more and more frequently.

Role specialization means that as companies grow, there are fewer and fewer people who know everything, and more and more people who just know their specialty. A business person who knew the entire order and fulfillment process fifteen years ago might only be required to know the order-to-cash process today. As a result, few people know the "big picture" today, causing communication issues sometimes even within the same department.

Tainted thinking means that some business professionals equate how they do their jobs to the software they use. And software changes much more frequently than business processes change, causing business professionals to continuously

> *rethink business processes. For example, if Bob explains the order-to-cash process with phrases such as "First I log into System XYZ and then click here to check credit terms," and System XYZ is replaced with another system, the business process may remain the same, yet from Bob's view it will most certainly change.*

The flow of the book generally alternates between two domains, the real world and computers. Chapter 1 is in the world of real information, exploring some enigmas in our concepts of "entities." Chapter 2 briefly visits the realm of computers, dealing with some general characteristics of formally structured information systems. This gives us a general idea of the impact the two domains have on each other. Chapters 3 through 6 then address other aspects of real information. Chapters 7 and 8, dealing with data processing models, bring us back to the computer. We top it all off with a smattering of philosophical observations in Chapter 9.

This has been an approximate characterization—one view—of what the rest of the book contains. Please read on to discover what you might think the book is about.

I want to thank the people who took the time to comment on (and often contribute to) earlier versions of this material, including Marilyn Bohl, Ted Codd, Chris Date, Bob Engles, Bob Griffith, Roger Holliday, Lucy Lee, Len Levy, Bill McGee, Paula Newman, and Rich Seidner. George Kent, of the Political Science Department at the University of Hawaii, provided a valuable perspective from a vantage point outside of the computing profession. Karen Takle Quinn, our head librarian, was immensely helpful in tracking down many references. I thank Willem Dijkhuis of North Holland for his substantial encouragement in the publication of this book.

And very special thanks go to my wife, Barbara, who helped make the book more readable, and who coped and sacrificed more than anyone else for this book.

Steve's Takeaways

- A map simplifies a complex geographic landscape in the same way that a data model simplifies a complex information landscape.

- A data model is a set of symbols and text that precisely explains a subset of real information to improve communication within the organization and thereby lead to a more flexible and stable application environment.

- We are looking at real information as it occurs in the interactions among people, but always with a view toward modeling that information in a computer-based system.

- Data models present a simplified view at the expense of not showing everything outside of data, such as process.

- "We do not, it seems, have a very clear and commonly agreed upon set of notions about data—either what they are, how they should be fed and cared for, or their relation to the design of programming languages and operating systems." True in 1967, and still true today.

- Beware the information technology/business gap that exists in many organizations. It can be due at least partly to our outdated beliefs in technology and information.

- The issues around the semantics of data become bigger when a computer system is involved because of systems complexity, role specialization, and tainted thinking.

"Entities are a state of mind. No two people agree on what the real world view is."

Metaxides

An information system (e.g., database) is a model of a small, finite subset of the real world. (More or less—we'll come back to that later.) We expect certain correspondences between constructs inside the information system and in the real world. We expect to have one record in the employee file for each person employed by the company. If an employee works in a certain department, we expect to find that department's number in that employee's record.

So, one of the first concepts we have is a correspondence between things inside the information system and things in the real world. Ideally, this would be a one-to-one correspondence, i.e., we could identify a single construct in the information system which represented a single thing in the real world.

Even these simple expectations run into trouble. In the first place, it's not so easy to pin down what construct in the information system will do the representing. It might be a record (whatever that means), or a part of one, or several of them, or a catalog entry, or a subject in a data dictionary, or.... For now let's just call that thing a *representative* and come back to that topic later. Let's explore instead how well we really understand what it is that we want represented.

As a schoolteacher might say, before we start writing data descriptions let's pause a minute and get our thoughts in order. Before we go charging off to design or use a data structure, let's think about the information we want to represent. Do we have a very clear idea of what that information is like? Do we have a good grasp of the semantic problems involved?

> *The book **The Hitchhiker's Guide to the Galaxy** should be required reading for both business and information technology professionals. Although this is a science fiction book, I believe parts of it are based in reality. At one point in the book, citizens on a planet millions of miles away from Earth decide to build the smartest computer. When they are done building this computer, it occupies the space of an entire city. After they turn on this computer, called Deep Thought, and it boots up, the first question they asked Deep Thought is, "What is the answer to life, the universe, and everything?" The computer responds in a monotone voice, "I will get back to you on that one," and then seven and a half million years later, spits out the number "42." The rest of the book, and the subsequent books in the series that followed, are all about trying to uncover why "42" is the answer to the meaning of life.*
>
> *"What is the answer to life, the universe, and everything?" is a lousy business question! Where are the business requirements? What really do these citizens want to know? It is not clear. Even Deep Thought responds, after announcing the number 42, with the comment, "I think the problem, to be quite honest with you, is that you've never actually known what the question is."*
>
> *We do this all the time. Instead of taking the time to understand the business requirements, we throw hardware and software at the problem. "Let's see, we have a large integration issue, let's buy this Enterprise Resource Planning system to solve it for us." The software doesn't solve the problem for us—we still have to do the hard part of resolving the integration issues, and then the ERP system can store this integrated state for us. Instead of finding out the business requirements for a business intelligence application, we search for existing reporting tools, thinking this may solve the problem. The solution, however, is to do the very difficult task of eliciting requirements from the business and figuring out what really needs to be built! So on your projects, continuously ask yourself what Kent asked us several paragraphs back: "Do we have a good grasp of the semantic problems involved?"*

Becoming an expert in data structures is like becoming an expert in sentence structure and grammar. It's not of much value if the thoughts you want to express are all muddled.

The information in the system is part of a communication process among people. There is a flow of ideas from mind to mind; there are translations along the way, from concept to natural languages to formal languages (constructs in the machine system) and back again. An observer of, or participant in, a certain process recognizes that a certain person has become employed by a certain department. The observer causes that fact to be recorded, perhaps in a database, where someone else can later interrogate that recorded fact to get certain ideas out of it. The resemblance between the extracted ideas and the ideas in the original observer's mind does not depend only on the accuracy with which the messages are recorded and transmitted. It also depends heavily on the participants' common understanding of the elementary references to "a certain person," "a certain department," and "is employed by."

> *The flow of ideas is not unlike the game of telephone we played as children. The first child whispers a sentence in the next child's ear, and as this sentence goes around the circle from child to child, it changes more and more, to the point where the originating child hears their sentence completely changed, leading to laughter all around. There is usually no laughter, however, when different interpretations lead to unforeseen costs, lost opportunities, and loss of credibility and brand recognition. Read the front page of any major newspaper as proof of what different interpretations of the same flow of ideas can actually cost. It is critical to an application's success for the flow of ideas to progress with clarity and common understanding.*

One Thing

What is "one thing"?

That appears, at first, to be a trivial, irrelevant, irreverent, absurd question. It's not. The question illustrates how deeply ambiguity and misunderstanding are ingrained in the way we think and talk.

Consider those good old workhorse database examples, parts and warehouses. We normally assume a context in which each part has a part number and occurs in various quantities at various warehouses. Notice that: various quantities of one thing. Is it one or many? Obviously, the assumption here is that "part" means one kind of part, of which there may be many physical instances. (The same ambiguity shows up very often in natural usage, when we refer to two physical things as "the same thing," when we mean "the same kind.") It is a perfectly valid and useful point of view in the context of, e.g., an inventory file: we have one representative (record) for each kind of thing, and speak loosely of all occurrences of the thing as collectively being one thing. (We could also approach this by saying that the representative is not meant to correspond to any physical object, but to the abstracted *idea* of one kind of object. Nonetheless, we do use the term "part," and not "kind of part.")

Now consider another application, a quality control application, also dealing with parts. In this context, "part" means one physical object; each part is subjected to certain tests, and the test data is maintained in a database separately for each part. There is now one representative in the information system for each physical object, many of which may have the same part number.

In order to integrate the databases for the inventory and quality control applications, the people involved need to recognize that there are two different notions of "thing" associated with the concept of "part," and the two views must be reconciled. They will have to work out a convention wherein the information system can deal with two kinds of representatives: one standing for a kind of part, another standing for one physical object.

I hope you're convinced now that we have to go to some depth to deal with the basic semantic problems of data description.

We are dealing with a natural ambiguity of words, which we, as human beings, resolve in a largely automatic and unconscious way, because we understand the context in which the words are being used. When a data file exists to serve just one application, there is, in effect, just one context, and users implicitly understand that context; they automatically resolve ambiguities by interpreting words as appropriate for that context. But when files get integrated into a database serving multiple applications, that ambiguity-resolving mechanism is lost. The assumptions appropriate to the context of one application may not fit the contexts of other applications. There are a few basic concepts we have to deal with here:

- Oneness. What is one thing?
- Sameness. When do we say two things are the same, or the same thing? How does change affect identity?
- Categories. What is it? In what categories do we perceive the thing to be? What categories do we acknowledge? How well defined are they?

> *As analysts and modelers, on almost every project we face "oneness," "sameness," and "categories." Oneness means coming up with a clear and complete explanation of what we are referring to. Sameness means reconciling conflicting views of the same term, including whether changes (and what types of changes) transform the term into a new term. Categories means assigning the right name to this term and determining whether it is an entity type, relationship, or attribute on a data model.*

> *Consider "student" in the context of a university. Oneness involves coming up with a clear and complete definition for the term "student." Sameness involves reconciling the Admissions department and Alumni Affairs department definitions of the term student, which currently mean very different things. Admissions considers high school students that apply and students transferring from other universities to be students. Alumni Affairs considers only those students who have graduated from this particular university to be students. Categories involve determining whether student should be an entity type or a role that a particular person should play—that is, how student should be described on the diagram.*
>
> *An interesting note: When most people think "data modeling," they think categories. That is, how do we represent this thing on the diagram? In reality, this activity occupies a very small percentage of the data modeler's time. The process of getting to oneness and sameness requires almost all of the effort. In fact, in some organizations, the effort is so substantial that it is divided into separate roles, where a data modeler is responsible for oneness and a data architect is responsible for sameness.*

Oneness, Sameness, and Categories are tightly intertwined with one another.

ONENESS (WHAT IS "ONE THING"?)

Consider "book." If an author has written two books, a bibliographic database will have two representatives. (You may temporarily think of a representative as being a record.) If a lending library has five circulating copies of each, it will have ten representatives in its files. After we recognize the ambiguity, we try to carefully adopt a convention using the words "book" and "copy." But it is not natural usage. Would you understand the question "How many copies are there in the library?" when I really want to know how many physical books the library has altogether?

There are other connotations of the word "book" that could interfere with the smooth integration of databases. A "book" may denote something with hard covers, as distinguished from things in soft covers like manuals, periodicals, etc. Thus a manual may be classified as a "book" in one library, but not in another. I don't always know whether conference proceedings constitute a "book."

A "book" may denote something bound together as one physical unit. Thus, a single long novel may be printed in two physical parts. When we recognize the ambiguity, we sometimes try to avoid it by agreeing to use the term "volume" in a certain way, but we are not always consistent. Sometimes several "volumes" are bound into one physical "book." We now have as plausible perceptions: the *one* book written by an author, the *two* books in the library's title files (Vol. I and Vol. II), and the *ten* books on the shelf of the library which has five copies of everything.

Incidentally, the converse sometimes also happens, as when several novels are published as one physical book (e.g., collected works).

So, once again, if we are going to have a database about books, before we can know what one representative stands for, we had better have a consensus among all users as to what "one book" is.

Going back now to parts and warehouses, the notion of "warehouse" opens up another kind of ambiguity. There is no natural, intrinsic notion of what constitutes "one warehouse." It may be a single building, or a group of buildings separated by any arbitrary distance. Several warehouses (e.g., belonging to different companies) may occupy the same building, perhaps on different floors. So, what is "one warehouse"? Anything that a certain group of people agrees to call a warehouse. Given two buildings, they might agree to treat them as one, two, or any number of warehouses—with all perceptions being equally "correct."

IBM assigns "building numbers" to its buildings for the routing of internal mail, recording employee locations, and other purposes. One two-story building in Palo Alto, California, is "Building 046," with the two stories distinguished by suffixes: 046-1 and 046-2. Right next door is another two-story building. The upper story is itself called "Building 034," and the lower story is split into two parts called "Building 032" and "Building 047." IBM didn't invent the situation. The designations correspond to three different postal addresses: 1508, 1510, and 1512 Page Mill Road are all in the same building.

Another IBM location in the hills of San Jose, California, is apparently one building, since it has one building number. The structure has eight distinct towers. Signs inside direct you to "Building A," "Building B," etc. How many buildings are there?

"Street" is another ambiguous term. What is one street? Sometimes the name changes; that is, different segments along the same straight path have different names. Based on a comparison of addresses, we would probably surmise that people on those various segments lived on different streets. On the other hand, different streets in the same town may have the same name. Now what does an address comparison imply?

Is a street terminated by city, county, state, or national boundaries? Suppose the street just ran right across the boundary, same name and all. Would you be inclined to say that people living in different countries lived on the same street?

Does the term "street" imply that motor vehicles can drive on it? Some are narrower than alleys, and some are pedestrian malls.

Does the term "street" include freeways, highways, thruways, expressways, tollways, parkways, autobahns, autopistes, autostradas, autoroutes, dual carriageways, motorways? (I'm really just trying to convey one idea—what do they call it in your neighborhood?) Very often, one highway will coincide with portions of many different streets along its route. Does a highway name count as a street name? Along some segments, the highway name might be the only street name. Various street segments will have various multitudes of names ("look at all the highway markers on that pole!"). And, after I make a turn, whether or not I'm on the "same street" may depend on my own state of mind: which street name did I think I was following? Finally: if I drive from Illinois to California on Highway 66, have I been on the same street all the way?

Thus, the boundaries and extent of "one thing" can be very arbitrarily established. This is even more so when we perform "classification" in an area that has no natural sharp boundaries at all. The set of things that human beings know how to do is infinitely varied, and changes from one human being to another in the most subtle and devious ways. Nonetheless, the "skills" portion of a personnel database asserts a finite number of arbitrary skill categories, with each skill being treated as one discrete thing, i.e., it has one representative. The number and nature of these skills is very arbitrary (i.e., they do not correspond to natural, intrinsic boundaries in the real world), and they are likely to be different in different databases. Thus, a "thing" here is a very arbitrary segment partitioned out of a continuum. This applies also to the set of subjects in a library file or information retrieval system, to the set of diseases in a medical database, to colors, etc.

This classification problem underlies the general ambiguity of words. The set of concepts we try to communicate about is infinite (and non-denumerable in the most mind-boggling sense), whereas we communicate using an essentially finite set of words. (For this discussion, it suffices just to think about nouns.) Thus, a word does not correspond to a single concept, but to a cluster of more or less related concepts. Very often, the use of a word to denote two different ideas in this cluster can get us into trouble.

A case in point is the word "well," as used in the data files of an oil company. In their geological database, a "well" is a single hole drilled in the surface of the earth, whether or not it produces oil. In the production database, a "well" is one or more holes covered by one piece of equipment, which has tapped into a pool of oil. The oil company had trouble integrating these databases to support a new application: the correlation of well productivity with geological characteristics.

SAMENESS (HOW MANY THINGS IS IT?)

A single physical unit often functions in several roles, each of which is to be represented as a separate thing in the information system. Consider a database maintaining scoring statistics for a soccer team, both on a position basis and on an individual basis. The database might have representatives for 36 things: 11 positions and 25 players. When Joe Smith, playing halfback, scores a goal, the data about two things is modified: the number of goals by Joe Smith, and the number of goals by a halfback. That human figure standing on the field is represented as (and is) two things: Joe Smith and a halfback.

Consider the question of "sameness." Suppose Joe switches to fullback, and scores another goal. Did the same thing make those two goals? Yes: Joe Smith made both. No: one was made by a halfback, the other by a fullback.

Why is that human figure perceived and treated as two things, rather than one or three or ninety-eight? Not by any natural law, but by the arbitrary decision of some human beings, because the perception was useful to them, and corresponded to the kinds of information they were interested in maintaining in the system.

If the file only had data about player positions, then the same physical object would be treated as being different things at different times. Joe is sometimes a halfback and sometimes a fullback. From the perspective of this file, his activities are being performed by two different entities.

Also consider two related people (e.g., husband and wife) who work for the same company. When considering medical benefits, each of these people has to be considered twice: once as an employee, and once as a dependent of an employee. How many people are involved?

Or suppose a person held two jobs with the company, on two different shifts. Does that signify one or two employees? Shipping clerk John Jones and third-shift computer operator John Jones might be the same person. Does it matter? Sometimes.

It is plausible (bizarre, perhaps, but plausible) to view a certain employee and a certain stockholder as two different things, between which there happens to exist the *relationship* that they are embodied in the same person. There would then exist two representatives in the system, one for the employee and one for the stockholder. It's perfectly all right, so long as users understand the implications of this convention (e.g., deleting one might not delete the other).

Transportation schedules and vehicles offer other examples of ambiguities, in the use of such terms as "flight" and "plane" (even if we ignore the other definitions of "plane" having nothing to do with flying machines). What does "catching the same plane every Friday" really mean? It may or may not be the same physical airplane. But if a mechanic is scheduled to service the same plane every Friday, it had better be the same physical airplane. And another thing: if two passengers board a plane together in San Francisco, with one holding a ticket to New York and the other a ticket to Amsterdam, are they on the same flight?

Classification, e.g., of skills, impacts the notion of "sameness" as much as the notion of "how many." The way we partition skills determines both how many different things we recognize in this category, and when we will judge two things to be the same. Consider a group of people who know how to do such things as paint signs on doors, paint portraits, paint houses, draw building blueprints, draw wiring diagrams, etc. One classifier might judge that there is just *one* skill represented by all of these capabilities, namely "artist," and that every person in this group had the *same* skill. Another classifier might claim there are *two* skills here, namely painting and drawing. Then the sign painter has the same skill as the portrait painter, but not the blueprint drawer. And so on.

The same game can be played with colors. Two red things are the same color. What if one is crimson and the other scarlet?

The perceptive reader will have noticed that two kinds of "how many" questions have been intermixed in this section. At first we were exploring how many *kinds* of things something might be perceived to be. But occasionally we were trying to determine whether we were dealing with one or several things of a given kind. And analogously, much of the fuss in many insurance claims and court battles revolves around determining whether several things relate to the "same" illness or injury.

Change

And then there's change. Even after consensus has been reached on what things are to be represented in the information system, the impact of change must be considered. How much change can something undergo and still be the "same thing"? At what point is it appropriate to introduce a new representative into the system, because change has transformed something into a new and different thing?

The problem is one of identifying or discovering some essential invariant characteristic of a thing, which gives it its identity. That invariant characteristic is often hard to identify, or may not exist at all.

We seem to have little difficulty with the concept of "one person" despite changes in appearance, personality, capabilities, and, above all, chemical composition. (The proportions and structure—i.e., the chemical formulas—may not change much, but the individual atoms and molecules are continually being replaced...again illustrating an ambiguity between "same kind" and "same instance": how rapidly is the chemical composition of your body changing?) When we speak of the same person over a period of time, we certainly are not referring to the same ensemble of atoms and molecules. What then is the "same person"? We can only appeal to some vague intuition about the "continuity" of—something—through gradual change. The concept of "same person" is so familiar and obvious that it is absolutely irritating not to be able to define it. Definitions in terms of "soul" and "spirit" may be the only true and humanistic concepts, but, significantly, we don't know how to deal with them in a computer-based information system. It is only when the notion of "person" is pushed to some limit do we realize how imprecise the notion is. This is the basis of some legal issues.

Modern medicine is dissecting our concept of "person" via transplanted and artificial limbs and organs. The Hopi Indians consider mental activity to be in the heart [Whorf]; they might argue that the recipient of a heart transplant becomes the person who the donor was—the donor has merely acquired a new body. (Is it a heart transplant or a body transplant?) We are more likely to take that position with respect to the brain, rather than the heart. A number of legal issues will have to be resolved when brain transplants begin to be performed (and the issues may get more complex if just portions of the brain are transplanted).

In an information system maintaining data about people, we will have to decide which information gets interchanged between two representatives. Which information is to be associated with the body, and which with the brain? A name? A spouse? Other relatives? How is the medical history rearranged? Who has which job? Skills? Financial obligations?

An analogous situation exists with automobiles. Suppose you and I start trading parts of our cars—tires, wheels, transmissions, suspensions, etc. At some point we will have exchanged cars, in the sense that the Department of Motor Vehicles must change their records as to who owns which car—but when? What is the "thing" which used to be my car, and when did you acquire it? The Department of Motor Vehicles (at least in California, I believe) has made an arbitrary decision: the "essence" of a car is the engine block, which is (they assume) indivisible and is uniquely numbered. Owning and registering a car is defined to mean owning and registering the engine block. All the other parts of the car can be removed or replaced without altering the identity of the car.

> *When does a thing change to the point that it is no longer the same thing and is now a new thing? These same issues are still relevant today, perhaps even more so because of amazing advances in science and technology. Several years ago I experienced firsthand the ambiguity between one thing changing yet still being that same thing, versus one thing changing to the point where it becomes a new thing. I was about to go for a run on the beach when my daughter (then four years old) asked, "Daddy, can you bring me back some shells? It's okay if the shell is chipped or missing a piece, but I don't want any shell pieces." Although it was easy for her to distinguish a chipped shell from a shell piece, I had a much more difficult time separating the two while jogging along the beach. Where do we draw the line between a chipped shell and a shell piece? That is, at what point does a shell change so dramatically that it is no longer a shell but now a piece of a shell?*

The same kinds of questions apply to organizations, such as companies, departments, teams, government agencies, etc. Is it still the same company after changes in employees? (Of course.) Management? (Yes.) Owners? (Maybe.) Buildings and facilities? (Yes.) Locations? (Probably.) Name? (Probably). Principal business? (Maybe.) State and country of incorporation? (Maybe.) The answers are significant to the handling of old contracts and other obligations, the determination of employee vacation and retirement benefits, etc.

And political boundaries. A database of population statistics must have some definition of what is meant by India, Pakistan, Germany, Czechoslovakia, etc., over time. There's more involved than a change of name; the things themselves have been created, destroyed, merged, split, re-partitioned, etc. In some other database, it may have to be understood that two people born at different times in the same town might have been born in different countries.

There are some kinds of change which result in the existence of two copies of the thing, corresponding to the states before and after the change. There are several ways to deal with this situation: (1) Discard the old and let the new replace it, so that it is really treated as a change and not as a new thing; (2) Treat the old and the new as two clearly distinct things; and (3) Try to do both.

> *Managing the existence of two or more copies or variations of the same thing occurs so frequently in business intelligence applications, that there is a term for this: "slowly changing dimensions" (SCDs for short). There are three types of SCDs. Should we overwrite the old information and just maintain the most current information (a Type 1 SCD), store all changes (a Type 2 SCD), or store some of the changes such as the most current and most recent (a Type 3 SCD)?*

The Murderer and the Butler

Combining the ideas of our last two sections: sometimes it is our perception of "how many" which changes. Sometimes two distinct entities are eventually determined to be the same one, perhaps after we have accumulated substantial amounts of information about each.

At the beginning of a mystery, we need to think of the murderer and the butler as two distinct entities, collecting information about each of them separately. After we discover that "the butler did it," have we established that they are "the same entity"? Shall we require the modeling system to collapse their two representatives into one? I don't know of any modeling system which can cope with that adequately.

> *We can model a Person playing multiple roles such as Butler and Murderer. For example, in the figure below, each Person may play one or many Roles, and each Role must be played by one Person. Each Role can be a either a Butler or Murderer.*
>
> *However, once we identify that Bob the Person playing the role of a Butler is the same person as Robert the Person playing the role of Murderer, how do we consolidate these two views into one person playing two roles? Although the model can depict such an idealistic view post data clean-up, work remains to make the data fit this clean view. The data clean-up activity is frequently extremely time-consuming and tedious.*

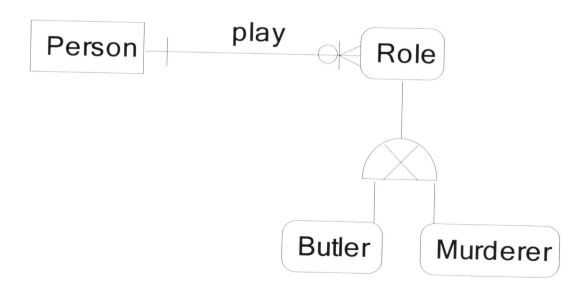

CATEGORIES (WHAT IS IT?)

We have so far been focusing on the questions of "oneness" and "sameness." That is, given that you and I are pointing to some common point in space (or we think we are), and we both perceive something occupying that space (perhaps a human figure), how many "things" should that be treated as in the information system? One? Many? Part of a larger thing? Or not a thing at all?

And: do we really agree on the composition and boundary of the thing? Maybe you were pointing at a brick, and I was pointing at a wall.

And: if we point to that same point in space tomorrow (or think we are), will we agree on whether or not we are pointing at the same thing as we did today?

None of this focuses on what the thing *is*. I don't mean its properties, like is it solid, or is it red, or how much does it weigh, but what *is* it? I had to use the phrase "human figure" above because I didn't think you would follow my point if I kept using the indefinite word "thing"—I had to convey some kind of tangible example. But that phrase is just one possible perception of the "thing" we pointed to. You might have said it was a mammal, or a man, or a solid object, or a bus driver, or your father, or a stockholder, or a customer, or...ad nauseam.

I will refer to what a thing is—or at least what it is described to be in the information system—as its "category," agreeing with the usage in, e.g., [Abrial]. The same idea is also often called "type," or "entity type"[4]. Like everything else, the treatment of categories requires a number of arbitrary decisions to be made.

There is no natural set of categories. The set of categories to be maintained in an information system must be specified for that system. In one system it might be employees and customers, in another it might be employees and dependents, or enrolled computer users, or plaintiffs and defendants, and in an integrated database it might include all of these. A given thing (representative) might belong to many such categories.

Not only are there different kinds of categories, but categories may be defined at different levels of refinement. One application might perceive savings accounts and loan accounts as two categories, while another perceives the single category of accounts, with "savings" or "loan" being a property of each account. In another case, we might have applications dealing with furniture or trucks or machines, while another deals with

---

[4] The common term today of "entity" is really referring to an entity type or category.

capital equipment (assigning everything a unique inventory number). Thus, some categories are, by definition, subsets of others, making a member of one category automatically a member of another. Some categories overlap without being subsets. For example, the category of customers (or of plaintiffs, in a legal database), might include some people, some corporations or other businesses, and some government agencies.

It is often a matter of choice whether a piece of information is to be treated as a category, an attribute, or a relationship. (Which raises the question of how fundamental such a distinction really is.) This corresponds to the equivalence between "that is a parent" (the entities are parents), "that person has children" (the entities are people, with the attribute of having children), and "that person is the parent of those children" (the entities are people and children, related by parentage).

It's often difficult to determine whether or not a thing belongs in a certain category. Almost all non-trivial categories have fuzzy boundaries. That is, we can usually think of some object whose membership in the category is debatable. Then either the object is arbitrarily categorized by some individual, or else there are some locally defined classification rules which probably don't match the rules used in another information system. Just as an example, consider the simple and "well-understood" category of "employee." Does it include part-time employees? Contract employees? Employees of subsidiary companies? Former employees? Retired employees? Employees on leave? On military leave? Someone who has just accepted an offer? Signed a contract but not yet reported for work? Not only do the answers have to be decided according to how the company wants to treat the data, but perhaps the questions can't even be answered consistently within the company. A person on leave may not be an employee for payroll purposes, although he is for benefits purposes. Then the notions of category and property have to be reexamined again, to arrive at a set meaningful to all users.

As another example, consider the category of "cars," and decide if the following are included: station wagons, micro-buses, ordinary buses, pickup trucks, ordinary trucks, motor homes, dune buggies, racing cars, motorcycles, etc. What about a home-made contrivance in which a short pickup truck bed is hung out of the trunk of a sedan? An old bus converted to a motor home?

As long as we are traveling, answer this question: What's the difference between a motel and a hotel? (If you have an answer, you haven't traveled much lately.)

The editor of a collection is often listed as the "author" of the book. Did he "author" anything?

The category of a thing (i.e., what it is) might be determined by its position, or environment, or use, rather than by its intrinsic form and composition. In the set of plastic letters my son plays with, there is an object that might be an "N" or a "Z," depending on how he holds it. Another one could be a "u" or an "n," and still another might be "b," "p," "d," or "q."

The purposes of the person using an object very often determine what that object is perceived to be (cf. [Stamper 77]). I can imagine the same hollow metal tube being called a pipe, an axle, a lamp pole, a clothes rack, a mop handle, a shower curtain rod, and how many more can you name? A nail driven into a wall might be designated a coat hook.

In part, these observations illustrate the difficulty of distinguishing between the category (essence) of a thing and the uses to which it may be put (its roles).

> *When we work on projects spanning different systems or departments, it is recognizing the distinction between the "essence" and "its roles" that allows us to realize connections across an organization and perform integration to produce a more holistic solution. Separating the person Bob, for example, from the roles he plays as student in the Student Registration application, and instructor in the Employee Payroll application, allows a university to represent and recognize Bob as a representative of the category Person playing two distinct roles, student and instructor.*

And, like everything else, the category of an object can change with time. A dependent becomes an employee, and then a customer, and then a stockholder. A slab of marble becomes a sculpture. A piece of driftwood becomes a work of art—just by being found and labeled! An ingot of steel becomes a machined part.

Perhaps the easiest way out is to ignore the principles of continuity and conservation that we have learned since earliest childhood. It simply is no longer the same object. The sculptor does not "modify" the marble. He destroys the slab, and creates a sculpture.

The fundamental problem of this book is self describing. Just as it is difficult to partition a subject like personnel data into neat categories, so also is it difficult to partition a subject like "information" into neat categories like "categories," "entities," and "relationships." Nevertheless, in both cases, it's much harder to deal with the subject if we don't attempt some such partitioning.

For a closing amusement, do you remember "Who's On First"? Well, here's a variation:

> *"Which is bigger, a baseball team or a football team?"*
> *"A football team, of course."*
> *"Why's that?"*
> *"A football team has eleven players, and a baseball team has nine."*
> *"Name a baseball team."*
> *"The San Francisco Giants."*
> *"How many players do they have?"*
> *"About twenty-five."*
> *"I thought you said a baseball team has nine players."*
> *"I guess it's twenty-five."*
> *"Any twenty five baseball players?"*
> *"No, just the twenty-five on one roster."*
> *"If they trade a player, does that change the team?"*
> *"Of course."*
> *"You mean they're not the San Francisco Giants any more?"*

And so on.

Existence

In a record processing system, records are created and destroyed, and we can decide with some certainty whether or not a given record exists at any moment in time. But what can we say about the existence of whatever entities may be represented by such a record?

HOW REAL?

It is often said that a data model models some portion of the real world. I've said so in this book.

It ain't necessarily so. The world being modeled may have no real existence.

- It might be historical information (it's not real now). We can debate whether past events have any real existence in the present.
- It might be falsified history (it never was real) or falsified current information (it isn't real now). Fraudulent data in welfare files: is that a model of the "real" world?
- It might be planning information about intended states of affairs (it isn't real yet).
- It might be hypothetical conjectures—"what if" speculations (which may never become real).

One might argue that such worlds have a Platonic, idealistic reality, having a real existence in the minds of men in the same way as all other concepts. But quite often the information is so complex that no one human being comprehends all of it in his mind. It is not perceived in its entirety by any agency outside of the database itself. Or, although not overly complex, the information may simply not have reached any human mind just yet. The computer might have performed some computations to establish and record some consequence of the known facts, which no person happens to be aware of yet. It happens all the time: computers often record accounts as being overdrawn some time before any people are told about it. And even more obviously: that is precisely the point of doing hypothetical simulations by computer. The computer figures out who wins a simulated war game; in the interval between the computation and a person's reading of the output, this result is in the computer—but what person "knows" it?

Where is the reality that the database is modeling?

And what about fiction? The subjects of some databases are the people, places, and events occurring in fiction (literature, mythology). This again stretches the concept of the "real world" being modeled in a database. (Isn't fiction the opposite of reality?) But beyond that, it challenges certain premises about certain kinds of entities.

It is sometimes held that there are certain "intrinsic attributes" which all entities of a certain type must possess. For people, such attributes include birthdate, birthplace, parents, height, weight, etc. Does Hamlet have these attributes? Cities have a geographic location, an area, a population, etc. Does Camelot have these attributes?

Or shall we say instead that Hamlet is not a person, and Camelot is not a city?

Note that this situation is very different from a simple lack of information. It is not uncommon to say that we don't know a certain person's birthday, and to record it as "unknown" in the database. That implies the possibility of eventually discovering and recording what it is. Instead, we are questioning whether such characteristics exist at all.

To conclude, if we can't assert that a data model models a portion of reality, what shall we say that a database does in general? It probably doesn't matter. Once again, it seems that we can go about our business quite successfully without being able to define (or know) precisely what we are doing.

If we really did want to define what a data model modeled, we'd have to start thinking in terms of mental reality rather than physical reality. Most things are in the database because they "exist" in people's minds, without having any "objective" existence. (Which means we very much have to deal with their existing differently in different people's minds.) And, of the things in the database which don't exist in any person's mind, whose mental reality is that? Shall we say that the computer has a mental reality of its own?

HOW LONG?

Some kinds of entities have a natural starting and ending, and others have an "eternal" existence; creation and destruction aren't relevant concepts for them. The latter tends to be true of what we call "concepts"—numbers, dates, colors, distances, masses.

We could be perverse and wonder in what sort of Platonic sense such concepts have "always" existed. Did zero exist before some ancient Arab thought of it? Did gravity exist before Newton? Did the concept of television exist 50 years ago?

It doesn't really matter, for our purposes. We are not going to have to worry about creating and destroying such conceptual entities. Unless...you are a cosmetics company, "inventing" new colors every day...or a number theorist, computing certain numbers (e.g., the primes, or perfect numbers), and adding each one to a list as you "discover" it.

There are, at the other extreme, tangible physical objects that have a well defined finite period of existence, a beginning and an end. Creation and destruction are very relevant concepts here.

But notice that I hesitate to list examples. Beginnings and endings are often processes, rather than instantaneous events. We get tied up in our definitions of what entities are in the first place. Is it the whole thing when it's partially formed? The whole abortion controversy centers on this: does a person become a person at conception, or birth, or somewhere in between? Does a car stop being a car when it enters the junkyard? Or after it's been deformed into a solid cube?

The entity concept enters in some other ways, too. Depending on what entity categories we choose, a certain process may or may not create an entity. Hiring merely alters the attributes of a person, but it creates an employee (but be careful—it might be a re-hire!). And, did the sculpture always exist in the marble? Recall the old vaudeville directions for sculpting an elephant: just cut away the parts that don't look like an elephant. In spite of all of this, we can entertain a notion that tangible objects have a finite existence, a beginning and an ending.

Not that we always really care. For most of our practical purposes, we prefer to treat certain objects as eternal, those whose "finite" existences appear virtually infinite: the continents, the planets, the sun, the stars. The creation and destruction of these are real only to astronomers, and to science fiction fans.

But suppose that we had neatly defined tangible objects, with instantaneous beginnings and endings. Does that solve all the important problems?

We are, of course, not interested primarily in the objects themselves, but in the information we have about them. Does our handling of this information mimic the creation and destruction of such objects? Do we start having information about such objects at the instant of their creation, and stop having the information at the instant of their destruction? Of course not. We often become aware of things long after their creation (the people we deal with, the things we buy). And we're sometimes aware of them before their creation. Data are kept about children before their birth. Unborn— and unconceived—children are mentioned in wills. Data may be kept about ordered merchandise long before manufacture begins.

And we certainly keep information about things long after they have ceased to exist.

So, does the creation and destruction of information have any direct relationship to the beginning and ending of objects? Almost never. "Create" and "destroy," when applied to information, really instruct the system to "perceive" and "forget."

Once more: we are not modeling reality, but the way information about reality is processed, by people.

Steve's Takeaways

- It is always easier (yet riskier) to attempt to solve a business problem through technology, rather than investing the effort to determine what the problem is by understanding people's perspectives and, ultimately, what they are looking for in an application.

- The information in the system is part of a communication process among people. There is a flow of ideas from mind to mind; there are translations along the way, from concept to natural languages to formal languages and back again.

- Oneness means coming up with a clear and complete explanation of what we are referring to. Sameness means reconciling conflicting views of the same term, including whether changes (and what types of changes) transform the term into a new term. Categories means assigning the right name to this term and determining whether it is an entity type, relationship, or attribute on a data model.

- At the beginning of a mystery, we need to think of the murderer and the butler as two distinct entities, collecting information about each of them separately. After we discover that "the butler did it," have we established that they are "the same entity"?

- When modeling, whose definition of "real world" is used and their perspective is very important.

- If we really did want to define what a data model modeled, we'd have to start thinking in terms of mental reality rather than physical reality. Most things are in the database because they "exist" in people's minds, without having any "objective" existence.

For the most part, we are looking at the nature of information in the real world. But our ultimate motivation is to formulate descriptions of this information so that it may be processed by computers.

The "ultimate motivation" of understanding the nature of information in the 1970s, 1980s, and most of the 1990s was to formulate descriptions and produce a data model that could be turned into a database for a new computer system. However, from the mid-1990s through today, many data modeling efforts are driven by trying to understand existing computer systems. If an application was originally built with minimal effort given to understanding information, and I will use the term "application" as a synonym for "computer system," eventually there comes the need to understand the information within this application. There are two main differences between representing the information for a new application versus representing the information from an existing application: process and filter.

The first difference is the process we go through. "Forward engineering" means driven from business requirements, and this is what Kent is referring to in the first paragraph of this chapter. Our goal is to understand information within the context of the business professionals so that we may build a useful application. The process involves interacting directly with these business professionals and collaborating on a solution. "Reverse engineering" means building a data model based upon an existing application. Often the driver behind reverse engineering is to replace or enhance the application because it was not designed properly. "Data archeologist" is the role we play when we reverse-engineer. Just as an archeologist must try to find out what this piece of old clay that was buried under the sand for thousands of years was used for, so must we try to figure out what these fields were used for when no or little documentation or knowledgeable people resources exist.

The Data Archeologist at Work

The second difference has to do with filter. When we are looking at information directly from business professionals or business requirements during forward engineering, the information we see and represent is pure business information. If a business analyst calls a thing a "Customer," for example, we would consider this thing to be a customer. When we reverse-engineer, however, this business information has been filtered through an application and therefore the information we see has been tainted. If an application calls a customer an "Object" or "Business Partner" for example, this is what we tend to consider this customer to be. So building on one of Kent's points from the prior chapter, forward and reverse engineering imply a different "context." Forward engineering is through the eyes of the business and therefore a business context, and reverse engineering is through the eyes of a specific application and therefore an application context.

In this chapter we briefly explore how the goal of formulating descriptions so that it may be processed by computers shapes our view of information. Among other things, we touch on the need for having data descriptions[5].

At a fundamental level, there are certain characteristics of computers that have a deep philosophical impact on what we do with them. Computers are deterministic, structured, simplistic, repetitious, unimaginative, unsympathetic, and uncreative. These notions I leave as background; that's a different plane from the one I want to be on. (Some may argue with those characterizations. Some artificial intelligence experiments have simulated more elegant computer behavior. But it remains an adequate description of the computers that will be processing our data in the near term.)

Data Description

In a totally generalized system, there might be a universal naming convention uniformly applicable to all things. For example, one might postulate that a name is any string of characters, of unlimited length; every thing has one or more such names (if several, the names are interchangeable and synonymous). Conventional systems don't support such generality, and we rarely want it. In most cases, there are restrictions on the kinds of names that are acceptable. There may be limits on length (perhaps a certain fixed length for a certain kind of thing), and restrictions on acceptable characters and syntax (only digits, only letters, must start with a letter, hyphens in certain positions, rules about blanks and commas and periods, etc.). A thing often has different kinds of names, which are not synonymous and interchangeable (Social Security number and employee number; license number and engine number). To enforce such constraints, we have to notify the information system, in advance, which naming conventions will apply to which kinds of things (to employees, departments, parts, warehouses, cities, cars, etc.).

Similarly, an information system might be totally permissive, imposing no constraints at all on the semantic sensibility of information. The system would accept such information as "the Accounting department has a shipping weight of 30 pounds, and has two children named 999-1234 and 12.50." While it is possible to build such totally generalized systems, it is customary, in all current data processing systems, to exclude such absurdities. Provision is needed to specify which things can sensibly have which properties, and which relationships make sense between which things.

---

[5] Data descriptions include all of the metadata, such as names, formatting, keys, and definitions. Metadata is defined as "Text that describes what the audience needs to see" [Hoberman 2009].

Pre-definition of information is also needed in order to specify security constraints, to specify validity criteria for information, and to specify how representations are to be interpreted (data type, scale, units, etc.).

There are also economic implications. Known limitations on the lengths of various information, and a predictability of which pieces of information will or won't occur together, make it possible to plan much more efficient utilization of computer storage. In fact, if the constraints are strict enough, very efficient repetitions of simple patterns can be employed. Furthermore, if formats are rigid enough, and the number of combinations of things that might occur is limited, then programs and procedures can be kept simple and efficient. This is precisely why data processing is currently done in terms of records.

Such rules and descriptions should be assertable before information is loaded into the system, and obviously can't be expressed in terms of individuals. ("Tom, Dick, and Harry must have 6-digit employee numbers.")

> *Kent, in this last paragraph, illustrates why we need to have entity types, attributes, and relationships. We need to plan ahead, just as we first write the column headings in a spreadsheet before filling in the values.*

At the semantic level, we have adopted (in Chapter 1) the term "category" to label the intrinsic character of a thing ("man or mouse"). It also offers an attractive way of specifying rules about things without referring to the individual things. One simply asserts that certain rules apply to all things in a certain category; one only has to name the category, not the individuals.

Categories are at the foundation of almost all approaches to the description of data, and we will also adopt such an approach for the time being. But we will have some critical things to say about it later.

> *Recall that a "category" is also known as an "entity type," and nowadays, less formally as an "entity," such as Customer, Organization, Role, Product, or Order.*

LEVELS OF DESCRIPTION

The various people and applications using a database are likely to have different perceptions of the entities and information they are dealing with (employees vs. stockholders; employer implied by record type vs. employer as a field value). Different applications use different facts about entities, so that an employee record may look quite different in the personnel application and in the medical benefits application. It is also possible for these applications to use different data processing disciplines, i.e., different file types, access methods, and data structures. These generally provide different ways of representing relationships and different interfaces for manipulating the data.

Thus there is a level of description corresponding to the perceptions and expectations of various applications, specifying such things as record formats, data structures, and access methods. For some kinds of question answering systems, or systems with graphical displays, the descriptions might not even be couched in terms of record formats.

All these applications may be supported by a common pool of data, an integrated database. One significance of integration is that common attributes are synchronized; e.g., changing an employee's address also changes his address in the stockholder file, if he happens to be one. Synchronization may be achieved by maintaining the address in only one place, or by the system's recognizing that a change in one place must automatically be propagated to another place. The method doesn't matter, as long as the information appears synchronized to users.

Another significance of integration is that a new application may "borrow" data already in the database for the benefit of other applications. The new application's requirements can be mapped directly to the integrated database. Without integration, it can be difficult and often impossible to extract the data from several physically unrelated files and then merge it into a form useful to the new application.

The integrated database is the system's analog to the real world: it is that ongoing persistent thing of which different applications may have different perceptions.

Although the integrated database is the system's analog to the real world, most attempts at modeling the entire organization fall short because they fail to acknowledge the many different perceptions. Not only do we need to build an enterprise data model showing how an organization should ideally be perceived, we also need to "map" each of the concepts on this holistic model to each of the different perspectives. For example, the enterprise data model might view Person as distinct from the roles that a person can play such as Employee and Consumer, whereas the Employee Payroll System only has knowledge of Employee and the Order Entry System only has knowledge of Consumer. To bridge the reality of different perceptions to the aspirational enterprise data model requires a mapping. This mapping is essential to any enterprise modeling effort. One can read an enterprise model and say "It's all very nice that a Person can play many roles, but where is my Consumer today?"

Unlike the real world, however, we don't have the luxury of merely saying "it's there—make of it what you will, with your own eyes and ears and mind." The database has to be described to the system.

We have a choice of describing the integrated database in "physical" terms, or in both "physical" and "logical" terms. Physical descriptions specify the location, format, and organization of the data on disks, tapes, or other storage media; the locations of key fields in records; the kinds of pointers used to reference related records; the criteria for physical contiguity of records, and the handling of "overflow" records; the kinds of indexes provided, and their locations; etc. Logical descriptions are more in terms of the information content of the database: the kinds of entities, the attributes, and the relationships among them.

> *There are conceptual, logical, and physical data models. Conceptual data models are the highest level and often do not exceed a single piece of paper in terms of their size. Conceptual data models are used to help scope projects and capture key concepts such as Customer and Product, along with their definitions. Logical data models are very detailed models that contain all of the attributes and relationships needed for the solution to the business problem. The physical data model compromises the logical data model mainly to make it work better with software and hardware tools, such as a particular database or reporting tool. So, the conceptual data model captures the business scope of the problem, the logical the business solution, and the physical the technical solution.*
>
> *Recall this model from earlier in the text. It is a conceptual data model:*

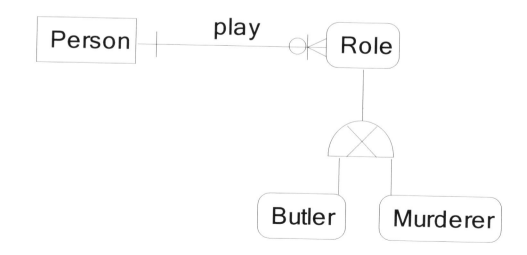

Adding all of the attributes, entity types, and relationships to this model produces the logical data model on the next page:

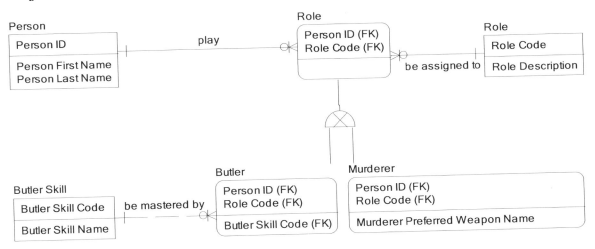

Considering technology may lead us to the following physical data model:

Butler

Butler_ID
Butler_Skill_Name
Butler_First_Name
Butler_Last_Name

Murderer

Murderer_ID
Murderer_Preferred_Weapon_Name
Murderer_First_Name
Murderer_Last_Name

*For a detailed description on how to read these models and the tradeoffs incurred from logical to physical, please refer to the book **Data Modeling Made Simple, 2nd Edition**.*

There is growing recognition of a need to provide and maintain these three levels of description ([ANSI], [GUIDE-SHARE]).

This separation into multiple levels of descriptions is necessary to cope with change. Experience has shown that the way data is used changes with time. Application programs change the way they use the data. They change record formats, and they change the combinations of records they need to see in a single process. New applications need to see records containing data that had previously been split among several records. Other new applications need extensions to existing data (e.g., additional fields in old records), without disturbing the old applications. Applications sometimes change the data management technique which they use to access the data. As an increasing number of applications interact with an increasingly large integrated database, the effects of such changes become much more complex, more difficult to predict and control.

A need is emerging to manage the data in a manner that is insensitive to such changes. A new role is emerging—the database administrator. A large part of his job consists of defining and managing this mass of information as a corporate resource ([ANSI] splits out this part of the job into the role of "enterprise administrator"). He needs a way to describe this information purely in terms of "what kinds of information do we maintain in the system." With this description (the logical model) as a reference, he can then separately specify the various formats in which this data is to be made available to application processes (the external models), and also the physical organizations in which the data is to exist in the machine (the internal model).

> *The 1978 role of database administrator has split into four roles over the last four decades: data modeler, data architect, database administrator, and database developer. The data modeler is responsible for translating the project business requirements into a data model. The data architect is responsible for ensuring consistency across data models—as Kent says in the paragraph above, for "defining and managing this mass of information as a corporate resource." The database administrator is responsible for maintaining existing databases so that they remain stable and perform well. The database developer is responsible for building new databases. In the 1980s and into the 1990s, there was also the role of a data administrator, responsible for maintaining the data models and other related metadata, such as data definitions. This role has largely been absorbed by both the data modeler and data architect roles.*

Besides its role in an operational database system, a logical model is also needed in the planning process. It provides the basic vocabulary, or notation, with which to collect the information requirements of various parts of the enterprise. It provides the constructs for examining the interdependencies and redundancies in the requirements, and for planning the information content of the database.

This book is essentially concerned with the logical model, i.e., the descriptions of the information content of the database. It reflects a perception of reality held by one person or group, in the role of database administrator. This administrator decides what portion of the real world is to be reflected in the database, and which constructs, conventions, models, assumptions, etc., are to be used. Although it is a single perception of reality, it must be broad and universal enough to be transformable into the perceptions of all the applications supported by the database.

THE TRADITIONAL SEPARATION OF DESCRIPTIONS AND DATA

In traditional record processing systems, constraints on information are implicitly enforced by the rigid discipline of record formats. The birthday of a car cannot be recorded anywhere, if there is no defined record format putting two such fields into one record. Alphabetic employee numbers are excluded by specifying the data type of the field as numeric; the defined field length determines the length of acceptable employee numbers.

Out of this practice emerged a "type" concept, referring to record formats. A set of records of type X all conform to the described format for type X records. And the systems require record descriptions. (But the level of discipline varies considerably. A system might only require specification of the length of a record, to know how to fit it into available storage. In such a minimal system, all kinds of junk might still be crammed into a record.)

> *Type includes both format (such as whether the attribute is a character or number), and length (such as a 15 character attribute or a decimal with five places before the decimal point and two after it). Often we make the type more precise by defining a list or range domain. A domain is the allowable set of values an attribute can be assigned. There are three main types of domains: type, list, and range. A type domain is limited to both format and length, a list domain is a specific set of values such as a business day of week list domain of {Monday, Tuesday, Wednesday, Thursday, Friday}, and a range domain is a range of values, such as between today's date and three months from now.*

Records and Representatives

An attempt to provide a regular modeling of the existence of entities leads to the notion of "representatives."

The traditional construct that represents something in an information system is the record. It doesn't take much to break down the seeming simplicity and singularity of this construct. What is a record? In manual (non-computerized) systems, it could be one sheet of paper, or one card, or one file folder. It might sometimes have a formal structure and boundaries, like a printed form (perhaps several pages long, or extending over several cards). Sometimes it doesn't have much structure, but runs on to several pages or cards (consider a library catalog that has continuation cards), yet with some recognizable convention for distinguishing one record from another.

The concept of "record" is equally muddy in computer systems. The term sometimes refers to:

- A geometrically defined piece of storage medium: card, record within a track on disk, area between blank portions of tape.
- A quantity of data transferred as one chunk between external storage media and main storage (sometimes called a block). This chunk of data generally goes into a buffer area in main storage, managed by an access method.
- A quantity of data transferred as one chunk by an access method between a buffer and an application program.

By various rules and conventions, we somehow know how to call a collection of data "one record" even though:

- It may physically exist in several copies (in main memory, on one or more auxiliary storage devices—e.g., a primary copy and a backup copy);
- It may not be physically contiguous (it may be stored in fragments, e.g., span tracks, on auxiliary storage);
- Its location and content change over time.

Thus, even at this level, we do not have a truly tangible, physical construct called "record," but rather we have to deal with it abstractly. We try to get by with some concept like "a record is that data which appears in my buffer whenever I submit a certain key to a certain access method using a certain index" (and even that is full of holes).

In some uses of the term "record," its characteristics are constrained by the processing system (device and media characteristics, access method) rather than by the information content appropriate to an application. This might include such constraints as:

- absolutely fixed length records (e.g., 80-byte card image).
- declarable but fixed lengths per "record type" or per "file."
- upper limits on record lengths.
- fixed number of fields per record.
- fixed length fields.

In general, the record concept grew out of data processing technology, and reflects many things besides the desire to represent an entity in a model of information. (More on this in Chapter 8.)

We are after some single construct that we can imagine to exist in the information system, for the purpose of representing a thing in the real world. Beyond grappling with the definition of "record," we have another traditional problem to contend with. In many current information systems, we find that a thing in the real world is represented by, not one, but many records. A library book is represented in the catalog by at least a title card, an author card, and a subject card. A person may be represented by a personnel record, a health record, a benefits record, an education record, a stockholder record, etc. In this latter case, of course, we are viewing all the files maintained by one company as constituting a single information system.

One objective of a coherent information system (i.e., an integrated database) is to minimize this multiplicity of records, for several reasons. In the first place, these various records usually contain some common information (address, date of birth, Social Security number); it takes extra work to maintain all the copies of this data, and the information tends to become inconsistent (sooner or later, somebody will have different addresses recorded in different files). Secondly, new applications often need data from several of these records.

So, we integrate these various records into one "pool" of data about an individual—and thereby introduce several new concepts of "record." On the one hand, it might be this pool of data. On the other hand, it is often used to mean that data which an application sees, which might bear no simple physical resemblance at all to the underlying pool of data. A "medical record" would consist of some subset of data out of this pool, perhaps collected from scattered physical locations, and formatted to the requirements of some application.

Well, then. If we can't pin down "records" to represent things in the real world, could we somehow use this underlying pool of data as a representative? Maybe. The problem is that we would like the representatives of two things to somehow be cleanly disjoint, to be distinctly separate from each other. Unfortunately, much of the data about something concerns its relationships to other things, and therefore comprises data about those other things as well. The enrollment of a student in a class is just as much a fact about the student as about the class. So, we can't draw an imaginary circle around a body of information and say that it contains everything we know about a certain thing, and everything in the circle pertains only to that thing, and hence that information "represents" the thing. Even if we could, the concept is just too "smeared"—we need some kind of focal point to which we can figuratively point and say "this is the representative of that thing."

We won't try to solve this problem. We will simply skirt the whole issue and continue to use the term "representative" (borrowing it from [Griffith]; [Hall 76] uses the term "surrogate"). We need the terminology to develop some concepts of information representation, without getting too tangled up in machine processing constructs. In some situations, a representative may correspond to a record or to a row in a relation; sometimes none of these constructs quite fits the concept of a representative.

Another reason for introducing the term "representative" is that our topic is broad enough to include systems that don't even use the term "record." In computer catalogs and directories, we have "entries," and in data dictionaries we have "subjects."

Although it is an abstraction, related to a theoretical view of data and data description, the representative has some definite properties, some of them reflecting the computer environment which is its ultimate motivation. The characteristics of a representative in an idealized information system might include these:

- A representative is intended to represent one thing in the real world, and that real thing should have only one representative in an information system. There may be some controlled redundancy in the physically stored data, such as duplicate copies of records in order to optimize different access strategies. That doesn't violate this principle, if there is some provision for keeping the contents of such records acceptably synchronized. Note that we have the corollary concept of information systems themselves as bounded, disjoint collections. Something in the real world may have several representatives in several information systems, but should have no more than one representative in each. Note further that this last constraint is a matter of intent, not definition. Something in the real world may in fact have several representatives in one information system, due to that system's failure to detect the duplication.
- Representatives can be linked. This is the fundamental basis for representing information (in addition to the fact that the representatives exist).
- The information expressed by linking representatives includes such things as relationships, attributes, types, names, and rules.
- The kinds of rules that generally need to be specifiable about representatives include conventions governing their type, names, existence tests, equality tests, and general constraints on their relationships to other things.
- The information associated with a representative must be asserted explicitly to the information system. The system is not omniscient[6]. (We exclude here

---

[6] Omniscient: "having complete or unlimited knowledge, awareness, or understanding; perceiving all things." Unabridged. Random House, Inc. http://dictionary.reference.com/browse/omniscient.

information that can be computed or derived from other asserted information.) The accuracy and currency of the information is determined by the assertions.

Steve's Takeaways

- "Forward engineering" means driven from business requirements, "Reverse engineering" means building a data model based upon an existing application. A "data archeologist" is the role we play when we reverse-engineer.

- We need to define entity types, attributes, and relationships anticipating future needs, similar to how we first write the column headings in a spreadsheet to accommodate the data that will be entered, before filling in the values.

- Conceptual data models are used to help scope projects, logical data models are used to capture the detailed business solution, and physical data models are used to capture the detailed technical solution.

- A domain is the allowable set of values an attribute can be assigned. There are three main types of domains: type, list, and range.

- The term "record" is ambiguous and its meaning is often determined by a particular context. For this and other reasons it is therefore better to use the term "representative" instead of "record."

- A representative is intended to represent one thing in the real world, and that real thing should have only one representative in an information system.

About half the time we spend modeling is spent eliciting requirements to build, replace, or enhance applications for the business. Most of this time is spent trying to represent our ambiguous world with precise descriptions. As you read Kent's words in this chapter, you can appreciate how much effort such an activity requires.

How Many Ways?

The purpose of an information system is to permit users to enter and extract information—about entities. Most transactions between user and system require some means of designating the particular entity of interest. In order to design or evaluate the naming facilities of an information system, it helps to be aware of the variety of ways in which we designate things.

How do we indicate a particular thing we want to talk about? Let me describe just a few of the ways I can think of:

- You point your finger. By itself that's generally ambiguous, unless there's something in the context or conversation to indicate whether you are pointing to a button, a shirt, the man's chest, the man, the horse and rider, or the whole regiment. Is this relevant? How about pointing a light pen at a display screen? If you are editing text, there has to be some way to establish whether you are erasing a letter, a word, a line, a sentence, a paragraph, or a letter (lovely ambiguity).

- If it's a person, you might use his name. Did I say "name," in the singular? There are many different sequences of letters and punctuation that are recognizable as his "name." There's his full name (with or without Ms. or Dr. or Capt. in front and Jr. or II or MD or Ph.D. in back); you might omit his middle name(s), or use only initials for either his first or middle names, or use only his initials altogether (monogram); you might use a nickname, or just the initial of his nickname (I sometimes get memos addressed to B. Kent, for Bill); you might address him only by his first name or nickname, or by his last name only; and in some cases you have to give his last name first. These are all, of course, ambiguous. People's names are generally non-unique. Whether you address a person by full name, first name, or nickname, there is always some chance that someone else will respond.

- Notice that I started that last discussion with "if it's a person." In identifying something, a name may be meaningless unless you also establish the category of the thing. What does the name "Colt" identify? It might be a person, a gun, a car, a beer, a football player, or perhaps even a city or county somewhere. (Check an atlas?) Of course, I'm being a little careless here. "Colt" is not the name of one gun or one can of beer or one football player. And, if it's not even clear that I am using a name, I might just be talking about a horse.

- A thing can have different kinds of names. A person might be identified by a Social Security number, employee number, membership number in various organizations, military service number, or various account or policy numbers (strictly speaking, these latter don't identify him, but something he's related to; on the other hand, you might also say that about a Social Security number). A car might be identified by license number or by engine number. A department may have a name (Accounting) and a number (Z99). A book has a title, a Library of Congress number, an International Standard Book Number (ISBN), not to mention various Dewey decimal identifiers in local library catalogs. So, to be complete, we may sometimes have to indicate the kind of identifier being used, in addition to the identifier itself and the category of the thing. Very often, but not always, the kind of identifier is implicitly understood (a Social Security number is generally recognizable by its format).

- You don't always have all these options. Very often you have to know who you're talking to; that will determine how you have to identify the thing being referenced. In addressing mail, you had better include the last name. For the Internal Revenue Service or a stockbroker, you might have to use a Social Security number. The personnel file might only be keyed on employee numbers. If the personnel file can be addressed by name, there are probably some very specialized rules, e.g., all capitals, last name first followed by a comma, truncate all names longer than 25 characters, etc.

- You might even have a choice of several different names of the same "kind" for the same thing.
    - A married woman often retains her maiden name for professional purposes. People have stage names, pen names, aliases, and sometimes several nicknames (Chuck and Charley).
    - A person's name may have several *correct* spellings, especially if it is transliterated from a foreign language. Look up the composer of "Swan Lake" in several catalogs.
    - When a book is published or distributed by different publishers (perhaps in different countries), then the book may bear several International Standard Book Numbers (ISBN). [Douque] is an example.
    - If you will accept a phone number as the "name" of a telephone, then we include the possibility of several names for the same instrument. The phone may also respond to several "kinds" of names: outside numbers and internal extension numbers.

- You might refer to someone or something by its relationship to another identified thing: Charley's aunt, Harry's car, the owner of a certain bank account or charge account. (How about "Mrs. Henry Smith"?) Such references may or may not be unique.

- Or by the role currently being played by the thing: the mailman, the bus driver, the third baseman.

- Or by its attributes: the red car, the highest-paid employee.
- And certainly by combinations of these: the red car's owner's lawyer. Again, these references may or may not be unambiguous.
- We often address a letter to a person when we really want to deal with his role (e.g., manager of a certain department). If someone else now has his job, we really want the matter handled by his replacement.
- A name sometimes describes the thing being named. Sometimes it doesn't. Main Street may or may not be the main street in town. Does Scotch Tape come from Scotland? How many blackboards are black? When my daughters were very young, they had a toy they called "Blue Car." It was a yellow donkey. (Or was it a toy, and not a donkey? Shall we debate whether the category of animals includes toys, pictures, statues, and other imitations of animals? Are you going to insist that the toy was not a donkey?) On television one night, the "8 O'Clock Movie" started at 7 o'clock. And then of course there are code names, which are deliberately uninformative or even misleading.
- Some names have embedded in them information about the thing being named. In some states, you can determine from a license plate the county in which it was issued, or the fact that the car belongs to a rental or leasing agency, or to a government agency. An account number often has the bank branch number included (this also relates to qualification). Prefixes very often have special meaning, as in the names of modules of computer programs.
- When dealing with ambiguity, we sometimes employ a complex strategy of reducing the number of candidates to one. Sometimes it is a pre-established strategy, e.g., specify name and address, or name and date of birth. Sometimes we do it in dialog fashion: "Is this the John Smith who works for IBM?" "Yes, but there are three." "Were you at the ACM meeting last week?" And so on.
- Sometimes we refer to something without knowing yet exactly which thing we are talking about. A mystery novel refers to "the murderer"; a contest announcement mentions "the winner." This is analogous to using variables in algebra and in programming. (It also bears some resemblance to roles, and to pronouns. In the case of roles, we are less likely to care about which individual is actually playing the role than when we use variable reference. The distinction between variables and pronouns does not so readily come to mind.)

Which of these phenomena shall we call "naming"? No answer. It doesn't matter.

Can we distinguish between naming and describing?

On one hand, there is a pure naming or identification phenomenon: a string of characters serves no other purpose than to indicate which thing is being referenced. On the other hand, we have information about the attributes of a thing and its relationships to other things. Of course, the two overlap.

There are very few "pure" identifiers, containing no information whatsoever about things. A person's name suggests possible relationships to other people; a first name can indicate a person's sex; a name often conveys ethnic clues; it may suggest something about age or social status; in some forms, it may indicate profession, or level of education.

> *Even a sequence number contains information about the thing being identified. For example, a counter assigned to each student when they enter the room reveals who entered the room first, second, third, etc.*

The serial number of a part often implies something about the date or place of its manufacture, or something about the presence or absence of certain features. Vacuum tube numbers encode much information about electrical and mechanical specifications. An International Standard Book Number (ISBN) encodes publisher, author, title, and type of publication.

What Is Being Named?

Which entity is being named? Consider telephones and telephone numbers (analogous to message handling in a message processing system). If, as before, we consider a phone number to be the name of a telephone, then:

- a telephone may have several names (several numbers ringing the same phone);
- a given number could ring several phones: the several extensions in your home, or the phones of a manager and his secretary;
- phones can change names (numbers): the phone company replaces a defective telephone, or the phone company assigns new numbers, or you transfer your number when you move.

> *To increase the potential ambiguity even further here, what is a "virtual" phone number, such as through Skype, naming?*

Alternatively, we could invent a new abstract entity, e.g., a "message destination" (in teleprocessing systems, a "logical unit"). We then consider one phone number to be the name of one message destination, and we deal with a *relationship* between message destinations and telephones (in teleprocessing, logical units and physical units). This relationship could be many-to-many, and can be changed. And it now requires some method for identifying (naming) the physical telephones involved.

> *As Kent stated, a very good use of abstraction is to create new concepts (such as "message destination") that mask the ambiguity of existing concepts. It may not solve the underlying data issues, but it will give us a "bucket" to put everything in, so eventually the data issues can be resolved by looking in one place.*

A familiar message again: you the observer are free to *choose* the way you apply concepts to obtain your working model of reality.

Uniqueness, Scope, and Qualifiers

Whether a name refers to one thing or many frequently depends on the set of candidates available to be referenced. This set of candidates comprises a "scope," and it is often implicit in the environment in which the naming is done. A reference to "Harry" is often understood to mean the Harry present in the room. A letter addressed to Portland (without naming the state) will probably be delivered in Oregon if mailed on the West Coast, and in Maine if mailed on the East Coast. The boundaries of a scope, and the implicit default rules, are often fuzzy: I don't know where the letter would go if it was mailed in Illinois.

> *Recall our earlier discussion on context. "What is the scope of uniqueness?" is a frequent question heard from the analyst or modeler. The broader the context, the greater the effort to integrate. If the Admissions department and Alumni Affairs department at a university each define "student" differently, modeling student just for the Admissions department is a much easier assignment than modeling student for the whole university including Alumni Affairs, as we would avoid the integration issues associated with multiple perceptions.*

Qualification, the specification of additional terms in a name, is often used to resolve such ambiguities by making the intended scope more explicit. In this case, adding the state name would (partially) resolve the ambiguity.

Scopes are often nested, and we often employ a mixed convention: a larger scope is left implicit, but a sub-scope within it is explicitly specified. This is partial qualification. There are cities named San Jose in Costa Rica and in the United States. Let's imagine that the one in Costa Rica is within a "district" named California. Then the address "San Jose, California," although qualified, is still ambiguous. Whether the letter gets to its intended destination depends on the "default scope" (i.e., country) implied by the point at which it is mailed.

Even the city name is a scope, resolving the ambiguity of a street address—University Avenue exists in many cities. And the street name selects a scope of house numbers. A complete address is a whole chain of scope qualifiers.

Telephone numbers provide familiar examples of qualification. A (7-digit) phone number is certainly not unique; it may exist within many different area codes. Here the boundaries of the scopes, and the default rules, are well defined. Incidentally, phone numbers illustrate some kinds of anomalies that may occur in real naming conventions:

- Different forms of names are valid within different scopes: for local extensions, they are four digits; for outside numbers, they are seven digits plus an optional area code.
- Form and content (syntax and semantics) are mixed together. You can't specify the naming rules independent of the numbers involved. Certain initial digits are reserved for certain functions. In the United States, if the first digit you dial is zero, then you are addressing the operator, not selecting a scope. Certain three-digit numbers are valid destinations, and not part of a seven-digit number (like 411 for information).
- The naming conventions can depend on the scope *from* which the naming is done: the phones at another location may have a different convention for getting outside lines, local extensions, etc.

DELIBERATE NON-UNIQUENESS

Quite often, things don't have individual unique names. This poses no problem when the things aren't individually represented in the system. In the case of parts, for example, we have one named representative for a type of part; the existence of individual instances is reflected only in the "quantity on hand" attribute.

Consider, however, something like a table of organization for a military unit. There may be several slots for clerks, with each slot having the same job description and skill requirements. We want them separately represented; they are the permanent entities in this structure. One of the *attributes* (or relationships) we want to record for them is the name of the person currently holding the position. When the positions are vacant, the information associated with the entities is identical. When we want to address one of them, e.g., to assign someone to a job, it is sufficient to refer to "any one of the vacant clerk positions." For this kind of information, the entities do not require unique identification.

It is sometimes asserted that each entity represented in the system must have a unique identifier. I contend that this is a requirement imposed by a particular data model (and it may make many things easier to cope with), but it is not an inherent characteristic of information.

> *As Kent says, the need for a unique identifier is imposed on us by the database management systems in use today, as well as performance requirements for getting to individual records quickly. Part of our job of organizing information is determining what makes an instance unique within each entity type. If we're lucky, the part has a Part Number, the employee has a Social Security Number, and the order has an Order Number. However, what we frequently find is that theoretically, these are the correct attributes for uniqueness, yet the actual information yields exceptions due to typing errors, obscure business logic, or unavailability of the information.*
>
> *On the other side of the spectrum, it is possible that there isn't a unique set of attributes for an entity type; in these situations, we often create what is termed a "virtual key." A virtual key is an attribute that is created by the data modeler to ensure there is something unique within an entity type when there is nothing real by which to retrieve an entity instance. That is, real in the sense of a true piece of business information.*

EFFECTIVE QUALIFICATION

Quite often, the technique for giving something a unique qualified name is simply based on an arbitrary relationship to some other object. In effect, the scope becomes the set of things having a particular relationship to a particular object.

Consider, for example, the naming of employees' dependents by the two fields consisting of the employee identification number plus the dependent's first name (the example is taken from [Chen]). In order for such a convention to be effective, a number of conditions must be satisfied.

Uniqueness Within Qualifier

The relationship must confer uniqueness of simple name within relative (i.e., the employee must not have two dependents with the same simple name). Curiously enough, even this might not hold for the given example. A pathological case would occur if the employee had several children with the same name (or is that in fact plausible with adopted children? or after remarriage?). More reasonably, his wife and daughter might have the same name, or his father and son (and grandson, if he was an eligible dependent).

> *Kent might have been surprised when boxer George Foreman named all of his sons George Edward Foreman—Jr., II, III, IV, V, and VI.*

Singularity of Qualifier

The relationship does not actually have to be one-to-many for naming purposes, so long as the previous constraint on uniqueness holds for each relative. Thus a person could be a dependent of several employees, and still be uniquely identifiable, so long as no employee has two dependents with the same first name.

However, this situation does give rise to synonyms: a given dependent could be identified by qualification by any of his related employees. This could lead to a number of problems, such as determining when two references to dependents were really references to the same person. And also: when a new employee lists his dependents, how shall we know if any of those dependents are already recorded as dependents of other employees? (Do we add new dependent records, or add synonyms to existing records?)

To avoid such problems, one could require that the identifier have no synonyms. Then dependents could no longer be identified via their related employees—unless we wanted to deny the reality that a person might be a dependent of several employees.

Existence of Qualifier

A qualifier must exist for each entity occurrence. Therefore the relationship must not be optional; each dependent must have a corresponding employee. If the benefits program were expanded, let's say as a charitable community service, to cover needy people unrelated to any employee, then this system of entity identification would no longer work.

Invariance of Qualifiers

Such a relationship must really be invariant (unmodifiable). The relationship constitutes information that is redundantly scattered about everywhere that this entity is referenced, with the potential for enormous update anomalies if the information can change. (Qualified names thus violate the spirit, if not the letter, of relational third normal form [Codd 72], [Kent 73].) Even this requirement might not be satisfied by the example cited. For tax purposes, two married employees might wish to change which one of them claims which children as dependents; such a change would have to be propagated into the qualifiers in every single reference to those children.

Scope of Naming Conventions

The oil well problem: some oil wells, but not all, have "API" codes assigned by the American Petroleum Institute. Oil companies assign their own names to the wells they own, using their own conventions and formats. Some wells are jointly owned, with each owning company naming the well according to its own rules.

In a database to be used for correlating data on all wells in some area, no single naming convention would apply to all the wells. The API code works for those wells that have them. Otherwise, you have to know who the owner is (or which owner's convention is being used, for jointly owned wells) before you know the applicable name format. When one company writes an application looking only at its own wells, it would like to see and use its own names. A second company's application would like to see and use that company's names, even when some of the same wells are involved.

The common solution: develop a brand new naming system (keys) for all wells represented in the database. Now everybody has to learn a new set of names, and correlate them with the ones they already know. And the headache will recur when several such databases are integrated.

Changing Names

Names do change: people, streets, cities, nations, companies, divisions, departments, programs, files, projects, books, other publications. Part numbering systems change once in a while. Mistakes get corrected.

In the references at the end of this book, SIGFIDET[7] and SIGMOD[8] are the old and new names of the same organization. Did you know that?

How (and how long) do you detect and handle references to the old names? Is this similar to synonyms?

The common solutions: either disallow name changes (pretend they don't happen), or generate a new naming scheme for the data system and treat the other (changeable) names as attributes. The latter solution has a price, of course: increased space required for storing and indexing the additional names, learning and processing problems in dealing with new, "unnatural" names; possible loss of "key" facilities of some access methods.

Systems that depend on symbolic associations for paths (e.g., the relational model), as opposed to internal "unrepresented" paths between entities, cannot readily cope with changing names [Hall 76]. That is a fact; we might, however, debate whether it is a fault or a virtue.

---

[7] Special Interest Group on File Description & Translation.

[8] Special Interest Group on Management of Data.

When name changes are disallowed by the system, one can trick the system by deleting the entity, and then inserting it again as a "new" entity under its new name. Unfortunately, it is sometimes very difficult, if not impossible, to discover all the attributes and relationships associated with the old entity, so that they may be re-established for the new entity. And sometimes deletion and insertion might have undesirable semantic implications of their own, enforced by the system and perhaps unknown to the application that is trying to change a name. This technique for altering an employee's identifier could enter a spurious firing and re-hiring into his employment history.

Versions

Quite often several versions of a thing are available, reflecting the status of the thing after various changes. The thing might be a document (e.g., various printings or editions of a book), a program, or a set of data records.

The central problem with the version concept is that we can't decide whether we are dealing with one thing or several. "The payroll program" is a singular concept, and a command to execute it is implicitly understood to refer to "the current version." On the other hand, one sometimes refers explicitly to an old version; for example, in order to reconstruct how a certain error occurred last month, one may want to rerun the version of the program that was current then. In this context, we are explicitly aware of the several versions as distinct entities, and have to specify the desired version as part of the naming process.

Names, Symbols, Representations

What is a name but a symbol for an idea? What essential difference is there between "Kent" and "25" and "blue," other than that they name different things?

Why Separate Symbols and Things?

DO NAMES "REPRESENT"?

In linguistics, a symbol is itself a representative of the thing it names. We have no choice; there isn't anything else. In the conventional linguistic view of verbal communication (written and spoken), including our normal communications with computers, we have nothing else except character strings to represent the things we are communicating about. This leads some people to conclude that we must use such symbols as the representatives of entities.

But in a modeling system, we do have an alternative. We *can* postulate the existence of some other kind of object inside a modeling system that acts as the representative (surrogate) for something outside the system. There "actually" is something in the system (a control block, an address in virtual memory, or some such computer-based construct) which can stand for a real thing. Once we've done that, we can talk about the symbols that name a thing separately from the representative of that thing.

Does this have any counterpart in our own experiences? Do we ever use anything besides words for communicating? Do we ever use pictures?

Consider the way we often use graph-like diagrams to supplement verbal communication, to help cope with synonyms and ambiguities in symbols. Our thing object is essentially a node on a graph, before any label has been written in it. We can decide what that node stands for before we write any labels; we then have a variety of options for choosing the label, and we may even change the label at various times. The same label might also occur on another node, but then we know it stands for something else. Or we might not write any label, because we can refer to it by its relationships to other nodes. But through all this, it is the node that has constantly been the representative of a certain thing, independent of the labeling considerations.

This is not to say that we can do without character strings. They are absolutely indispensable in describing and referring to what is being represented and linked. What we have done is to shift the primary responsibility for representing things away from character strings and onto a system of objects and links. Then we use character strings for description and communication. This shift of responsibility gives us greater freedom in how we use the character strings, and helps us escape a multitude of problems rooted in the ambiguity and synonymity of symbols.

This idea of taking the label out of the node, of treating an object separately from the various symbols with which it might be associated, should be exploited for a number of reasons:

- We can cope with objects that have no names at all (at least in the sense of simple labels or identifiers). We can support other ways of referring to an object, e.g., via its relationships with other objects.
- The separation permits symbol objects to be introduced and described (constrained) in the model, independent of the objects that they might name. One can thus introduce the syntax of data types, Social Security numbers, product codes, etc.
- Naming rules can be expressed simply in the form of relationships between thing types and symbol types.

- Other useful relationships might be expressed among symbols: synonyms, abbreviations, encodings, conversions.
- Various kinds of relationships might exist between things and strings:
  - Present name vs. past.
  - Legal name vs. pseudonym, alias, etc.
  - Maiden name vs. married name.
  - Primary name vs. synonym.
  - Name vs. description.
  - Which name (representation) is appropriate for which language (or other context). This could be useful in multilingual environments, such as the UN, the EEC, multinational corporations, and countries such as Canada, Switzerland, and Belgium.
- The structures of names can be distinguished from the structure of an object. For example, a particular day, such as the day on which you were born, is a single concept, a single entity. Its names, however, come in various forms. Most of the conventional notations take three fields; in Julian notation, however, it occupies one field. (And something else to think about: is the representation of a date in years, months, and days really all that different from representing a length in miles, feet, and inches?) Thus we should generally avoid confusing the structure of an object with the structures of its names.
- The separation permits differentiating between different *types* of names for a given thing, e.g., person name, employee number, Social Security number. Such types are themselves a normal part of the information structure available from the model.
- By distinguishing sets of things from sets of signs, we can avoid confusing several kinds of assertions:
  - Assertions about real things: "Every employee must be assigned to exactly one department."
  - Assertions about signs: "A department code consists of a letter followed by two numbers."
  - Assertions relating things and signs: "A department has exactly one department code and one department name."

SIMPLE AMBIGUITY

"It all depends on what you mean by ambiguity."

We mustn't neglect the plain and familiar ambiguities, which make their own large contribution to our communication confusion. Most words simply do have multiple meanings; we can't escape that. Some comments and corollaries:

- As evidence of the multiplicity of meanings, simply consider the average number of definitions per word in a dictionary. Then extend that to include all kinds of dictionaries, e.g., glossaries of specialized terms. Then add in the undocumented varieties of jargon used in various specialties. And include all the times a technical article begins by defining the terms it will use. And allow for variations in usage in different parts of the country, and in different countries. And slang, and metaphor.

- Ambiguity appears to be inevitable, in an almost mathematical sense, if we consider the relative magnitudes of the set of concepts and the set of words. The set of concepts that might enter our minds appears to be quite infinite, especially if we count every shade of meaning, every nuance and interpolation, as a separate concept. On the other hand, the number of words of a reasonable length (say, less than 25 letters) which can be formed from a small finite alphabet is quite small in comparison. It seems inevitable that many of these words would have to be employed to express multiple concepts.

- "...[F]uzziness, far from being a difficulty, is often a convenience, or even an essential, in communication and control processes. It might be noted that in ordinary human communications, the ability to stretch and modify word meanings is essential. There are many more situations occurring in life than we have ready-made tags for. Even so simple a word as 'chair' has all kinds of readily visible complexities in its use. It has *ambiguity*, in that it has more than one distinct area of application (in addition to the usual, we have 'Would the chair recognize my motion now?' and 'Would you like to chair this meeting?'). *Vagueness* (or fuzziness) is closely related to *generality*, the possibility of referring to more than one object. In fact, without generality, language would be almost impossible. Imagine if we had to give each chair a new proper name before we could talk about it! As far as *'stretchiness'* is concerned, note that some people make a living designing objects they call 'chairs,' but in which other people might sit with only the greatest reluctance. The concept of 'chair' is constantly evolving, in fact" [Goguen].

- The complexity of legal jargon testifies to the difficulty of being precise and unambiguous.

- Observe the number of puns and jokes that depend on ambiguity ("walk this way").

- If you listen carefully, you will discover all kinds of ambiguities occurring continuously in your daily conversations. If you listen too carefully, it could drive you out of your mind. Consider:

o When a receptionist directs you to "go through the same door as you did yesterday," she refers to doorway, not the door. Would you care if carpenters had replaced the door in the meantime? Or the doorframe?

o "Turn left at the second traffic light" means you should turn left at the second intersection that has traffic lights. The first such intersection probably has two traffic lights itself.

- Why should we expect the language which describes a customer's business to be any better understood or less ambiguous than the language which describes our own? Data theorists are ready to argue about any of the following words and phrases: data, database, data bank, database administrator, information system, data independence, record, field, file, user, end user, performance, navigation, simplicity, naturalness, entity, logical, physical, model, attribute, relationship, relation, set, integrity, security, privacy, authorization....

SURROGATES, INTERNAL IDENTIFIERS

Some alternative models suggest that some sort of an internal construct be used to represent an entity, acting as a "surrogate" for it ([Hall 76]). This surrogate would occur in data structures wherever the entity is referenced, and naming problems would at least be isolated by keeping structured or ambiguous identifiers off to one side, outside the structures representing attributes and relationships.

Since these surrogates must eventually be implemented inside the computer in some form of symbol string, it is sometimes held that such surrogates are themselves nothing but symbols.

It is useful to be aware of some fundamental differences between surrogates and ordinary symbols:

- A surrogate need not be exposed to users. Only ordinary symbols pass between user and system. In concept, models involving surrogates behave as though a fact (e.g., the assignment of an employee to a department) was treated in two stages. First, the surrogates corresponding to the employee and department identifiers are located (i.e., name resolution). Then the two surrogates are placed in association with each other, to represent the fact.
- Users do not specify the format, syntax, structure, uniqueness rules, etc. for surrogates.
- A surrogate is intended to be in one-to-one correspondence with some entity which it is representing. In contrast, the correspondence between symbols and entities is often many-to-many.

- Surrogates are atomic, unstructured units. That is, there is never a question concerning how many fields it occupies.

> *A surrogate key is a substitute for a natural key, used by IT to facilitate integration and introduce database efficiencies. It is usually a counter. The first entity created is assigned a surrogate key value of "1," the second one created receives a value of "2," etc. Also, it is important to note that surrogate keys are not always implemented as **globally unique**. Sometimes, they are just unique within a functional area or application.*

Sameness (Equality)

A counterpart of the existence test from Chapter 2 is the equality test. When shall two symbol occurrences be judged to refer to the same entity? (We mean "symbol" broadly in this context to include phrases, descriptions, qualified names, etc.) In general, different modes are applicable to different entity types. It is as much a specifiable characteristic as the naming conventions themselves.

TESTS

We can describe several kinds of equality tests: match, surrogate, list, and procedural:

- A *match* test is based on simple comparison between the symbols. They are judged to refer to the same entity if and only if the symbols themselves are the same (by whatever rule sameness is judged, with regard to, e.g., case, font, size, color, etc.). Addresses are typically treated in this way; any variation in the character sequence implies unequal addresses.
- In a *surrogate* test, each symbol is interpreted to refer to some surrogate object (e.g., a record occurrence). If both symbols refer to the same surrogate, the symbols are judged equal. (Following [Abrial]: "Equality always means identity of internal names.")
- A *list* test involves a simple list of synonyms. That is, they might indicate which color names are to be considered synonymous (crimson and vermilion might occur together in one company's list, but not in another's), or give the various forms of abbreviation for a given term. If the two symbols occur in the same list, they are judged equal.
- A *procedural* test involves some other arbitrary procedure by which the two symbols are judged equal. These are most often performed in relation to numeric quantities.

It is not generally acknowledged that equality tests for numeric quantities exhibit much the same characteristics as equality tests for non-numeric symbols. For numeric quantities, a number of factors are generally involved:

- The quantities are more likely to be judged equal if they were initially named by the same "conventions," i.e., measured and recorded with the same precision.
- The quantities need to be "converted" into common units of measure, data types, representations, etc. These are, in effect, replacing the original symbols with procedurally determined synonyms.
- Compare the two symbols. In many cases, the quantities only have to match within a certain tolerance ("fuzz") to be judged equal. This is another procedure for recognizing synonymous symbols, effectively similar to explicit lists of synonyms (considering crimson and vermilion to be equal is really a form of fuzz; to some people the difference in those two colors is significant).

There is certainly some interaction between the forms of the equality tests and the existence tests. Not all of the equality tests are applicable to entities subject to each of the existence tests.

FAILURES

When equality is based on symbol matching, several kinds of erroneous results can arise.

- If things have aliases, then equality will not be detected if two different names for the same thing are compared.
- If symbols can be ambiguous (name several things), then spurious matches will occur. Different things will be judged to be the same, because their names match.

(When qualified names are involved, another kind of spurious match can occur—see Chapter 8.)

These concerns are especially relevant when attempting to detect implicit relationships based on matching symbols. In general, when aliases are supported, we have to know:

- When two symbols refer to the same thing.
- Which symbol(s) to reply in answer to questions.
- Whether use of a new symbol implies a new object or a new name for an existing object.

Steve's Takeaways

- About half the time we spend modeling is spent eliciting requirements to build, replace, or enhance applications for the business. Most of this time is spent trying to represent our ambiguous world with precise descriptions.

- Can we distinguish between naming and describing?

- There are very few "pure" identifiers, containing no information whatsoever about things. Even a counter contains information about the thing being identified.

- A very good use of abstraction is to create new concepts (such as "message destination") that mask the ambiguity of existing concepts. It may not solve the underlying data issues, but it will give us a "bucket" to put everything in so that eventually the data issues can be resolved by looking in one place.

- Context continuously plays an important role. For example, in this chapter, "What is the scope of uniqueness?"

- The common solutions when names change: either disallow name changes (pretend they don't happen), or generate a new naming scheme for the data system and treat the other (changeable) names as attributes.

- Most words simply do have multiple meanings, leading to lots of ambiguity.

- A surrogate key is a substitute for a natural key. It is used by IT to facilitate integration and introduce database efficiencies.

- There are four kinds of equality tests: match, surrogate, list, and procedural.

Relationships are the stuff of which information is made. Just about everything in the information system looks like a relationship.

A relationship is an association among several things, with that association having a particular significance. For brevity, I will refer to the significance of an association as its "reason." There is an association between you and your car, for the reason that you own it. There's an association between a teacher and a class, because he teaches it. There's an association between a part and a warehouse, because the part is stored there.

Relationships can be named, and for now we will treat the name as being a statement of the reason for the association. As usual, we have to be careful to avoid confusion between kinds and instances. We often say that "owns" is a relationship, but it is really a *kind* of relationship of which there are many instances: your ownership of your car, your ownership of your pencil, someone else's ownership of his car. I will often (but not consistently) use the unqualified term "relationship" to mean a kind, and add the term "instance" if that's what is meant. So, to be precise, our opening definition was of a relationship instance. A relationship then becomes a collection of such associations having the same reason.

Note that the reason is an important part of the relationship. Just identifying the pair of objects involved is not enough; several different relationships can exist among the same objects. Thus, if the same person is your brother, your manager, and your teacher, these are instances of three different relationships between you and him.

> *I consistently remind myself that the verb name on the relationship in a data model must describe a good business reason. I try to use verbs such as "contain," "own," and "assign," rather than generic, less business-reason-centric terms such as "associate," "relate to," or "has." An Employee that is "associated with" one or more Customers provides less insight than an Employee who "visits" one or more Customers.*

Degree, Domain, and Role

We have so far looked only at relationship instances involving two things. They can also be of higher "degree." If a certain supplier ships a certain part to a certain warehouse, then that is an instance of a relationship of degree three. If that supplier uses a certain trucking company to ship that part to that warehouse, then we have a fourth-degree relationship.

We must distinguish between "degree" and a confusingly similar notion. If a department employs four people, we might view that as an association among five things. If another department employs two people, we have an association among three things, and we couldn't say in general that the "employs" relationship has any particular degree.

We proceed out of this dilemma in several steps. As a first approximation, think of a relationship (not an instance) as a pattern, given as a sequence of categories (e.g., departments and employees). An instance of such a relationship then includes one thing from each category (i.e., one department and one employee). The degree of such a relationship would then be the number of categories in the defining pattern. What we have done is to reduce the "employs" relationship from being an association between one department and all of its employees to being an association between one department and one of its employees. Although the former is certainly a legitimate relationship, it is difficult to subject it to any definitional discipline. We will only deal with relationships in the latter form.

It is also possible to think of the relationship between a department and all its employees as a relationship between two things, where the second thing is the set of employees in the department. This introduces a new construct, namely the *set* of employees as a single object, and the relationship is now indirect: employees belong to the set, and the set is related to the department. We will not pursue this alternative.

Specifying the pattern of a relationship as a sequence of categories is sometimes too restrictive. There are many relationships that permit several categories to occur at the same "position," as is the case when one can "own" many kinds of things. We therefore introduce the term "domain" to designate all the things that may occur at a given position in the relationship. A domain may include several categories. Thus we might describe an "owns" relationship as having two domains, with the first domain including such categories as employees, departments, and divisions, while the second domain included such categories as furniture, vehicles, stationery supplies, computers, etc.

"Domain" and "category" could be treated as the same concept if (1) we are dealing with a system which permits overlapping categories, e.g., unions and subsets; (2) the system does not impose intolerable performance or storage penalties for maintaining many declared categories; and (3) it doesn't bother our intuitions to think of all owners of things as a single kind of entity, and all owned things as another single kind.

One final improvement in the specification of relationships makes the specification more informative and less formally structured. Instead of assigning a domain to a sequential position in a pattern, we can give it a unique "role" name describing its function in the relationship, such as "owner" and "owned." Thus a relationship can be specified as an unordered set (rather than a sequential pattern) of unique role names. The number of role names is the degree of the relationship. A domain is specified for each role.

Role names are especially useful when several roles draw from the same domain. A "manages" relationship would be defined over the roles "manager" and "managed," both drawing from the domain of employees.

Forms of Binary Relationships

Much of the information in an information system is about relationships. However, most data models do not provide a direct way to describe such relationships, but provide instead a variety of representational techniques (record formats, data structures). Implicit in most of these, and in the accompanying restrictions in the data processing system, is the ability to support some forms of relationships very well, some rather clumsily, and some not at all.

In order to assess the capabilities of a data model, it would help to have some systematic understanding of the various forms of relationships that can occur in real information. In the next few paragraphs I will discuss some significant characteristics of relationships. A particular "form" of a relationship is then some combination of these characteristics. A method for assessing a data model would include a determination of which forms it supported well, poorly, or not at all. Note the emphasis on combinations. In most data models you can probably manage to find a way to obtain most of the following features, taken one at a time. The challenge is to support relationships having various combinations of these features.

By "support," I mean that

- the system somehow permits a constraint to be asserted for the relationship (e.g., that it is one-to-many), and
- the system thereafter enforces the constraint (e.g., will not allow the recording of an employee's assignment to more than one department at a time).

Such support is often implicit in the data structure (e.g., hierarchy), rather than being declared explicitly.

> *Note that Kent's use of the term "support" equates to today's term of "referential integrity."*

The set of characteristics listed below is probably incomplete—I imagine it will always be possible to think of additional relevant criteria. For simplicity, we are now only considering "binary" relationships, i.e., those of degree two. Most of the concepts can be readily generalized to "*n*-ary" relationships (those of any degree).

COMPLEXITY

Relationships might be one-to-one (departments and managers, monogamous husbands and wives), one-to-many (departments and employees), or many-to-many (students and classes, parts and warehouses, parts assemblies). The relationship between employees and their *current* departments is (typically) one-to-many, whereas the relationship between employees and all the departments they have worked in (as recorded in personnel history files) is many-to-many.

Another way to characterize complexity is to describe each direction of the relationship separately as simple (mapping one element to one) or complex (mapping one element to many). The terms "singular" and "multiple" are also used. Thus "manager of department" is simple in both directions; "manager of employee" is simple in one direction and complex in the other. Relative to the number of "forms" of relationships, this would count as four possibilities, since a given relationship might be simple or complex in each direction.

One advantage to this latter view is that it corresponds well with certain aspects of data extraction. Very often a relationship is being traversed in one direction (e.g., find the department of a given employee); the data processing system usually has to anticipate whether the result will contain one element or many (e.g., whether an employee might be in more than one department). The complexity of the reverse direction is of little concern (i.e., whether or not there are also other employees in the department).

Thus, if a given direction is complex, it doesn't matter much whether the relationship is 1:n or m:n. If the direction is simple, the distinction between n:1 and 1:1 may be immaterial.

It's amusing to note that the relationship between postal zip codes and states in the United States is *almost* many-to-one, so that the zip code directory is organized hierarchically as zip codes within states. The relationship is really many-to-many, but there are only about four zip codes that actually span state boundaries. The post office copes with that by listing the exceptions at the front of the directory.

CATEGORY CONSTRAINTS

Either side of a binary relationship might be constrained to a single category, constrained to any of several specified categories, or unconstrained (three possibilities on each side, for a total of nine combinations). Constraint to a single category is probably the most common situation, as in the examples above under "Complexity."

Constraint to a set of categories occurs, for example, when a person can "own" things in several different categories, or when the owner might be a person, department, division, company, agency, or school. This case might be avoided by defining one new category as the union of the others—if you're dealing with a data model which permits overlapping categories.

> *Also known as subtyping, this is when you define a generic concept called a supertype that contains all of the common properties of other entity types called subtypes. For example, the generic concept of Event might contain the common properties of different types of events such as Order, Return, and Shipment. Event is considered the supertype and Order, Return, and Shipment are considered subtypes.*

It is hard to think of a relationship that is naturally unconstrained as to category (i.e., one that applies to every kind of thing), but it often makes sense to handle a relationship that way in a real data processing system. Perhaps the relationship does happen to apply to all of the things represented in this particular database, or to so many of them that it isn't worth checking for the few exceptions. Perhaps the installation doesn't want to incur the overhead of enforcing the constraint, and trusts the applications to assert only sensible relationships. Or, the system simply may not provide any mechanism for asserting and enforcing such constraints.

SELF-RELATION

Three possibilities:

1. The relationship is not meaningful between things in the same category.
2. Things in the same category may be so related, but a thing may not be related to itself.
3. Things may be related to themselves.

The first case is again probably the most common. The second occurs, for example, in organization charts and parts assemblies. Examples of the third are our representatives in government (the representative is one of his own constituents), and canvassers for fund drives (the canvasser collects from himself).

Incidentally, I am thinking here of the simple case where categories are mutually exclusive. When categories overlap, as in subsets, things may be more complicated.

> *Self-relation is described on the data model through a recursive relation, which is a relationship that starts and ends at the same entity type. Recursive relationships allow for a lot of flexibility but come with the high price of reducing model readability and obscuring business rules.*
>
> *For example, in the following figure, we see two ways of modeling a sales organization:*

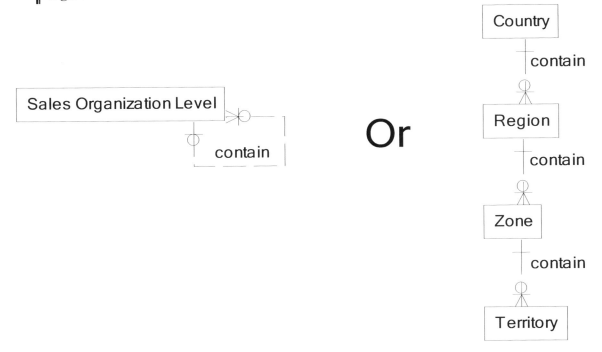

> *The entity Sales Organization Level related to itself (left) produces an extremely flexible structure, as we can have any number of levels and even gracefully change the rule that instead of a Zone containing Territories, a Territory now contains Zones. However, the cost for flexibility is often obscurity, as recursion hides business rules and makes it a more challenging communication tool. On the right, though, is the model without recursion. This model shows the four levels clearly. But if there is a fifth level, it would require effort to fix the model and update the resulting database and code.*

OPTIONALITY

On either side of the binary relationship, the relationship might be optional (not everybody is married) or mandatory (every employee must have a department). I will count this as four combinations (two possibilities on each side), although there could conceivably be more: one of the domains may include several categories, with the relationship being optional in some categories and mandatory in others.

THE NUMBER OF FORMS

Even with this limited list of characteristics, we already have 432 forms (4 x 9 x 3 x 4). This number might include some symmetries, duplicates, and meaningless combinations, but after subtracting these we still have a sizable checklist.

Other Characteristics

There are a number of other characteristics of relationships that might be worth describing to an information system. (We are still looking only at binary relationships.)

TRANSITIVITY

For some relationships, if X is related to Y and Y is related to Z, then X is automatically related to Z. This is true of ordering relationships (less than, greater than) and equivalence relationships (equal to, has same manager as). This characteristic is only meaningful when both domains of the relationship include the same category.

SYMMETRY

For some relationships, X being related to Y implies that Y has the same relationship to X. This is true of equivalence relationships and also, for example, "is married to." (In the latter case, both domains are "people." The relationship "is the husband of" between the categories of men and women is not symmetric.) Again, symmetry is only meaningful when both domains include the same category.

It's worth confessing that purely symmetric relationships only fit awkwardly into this general structure of relationships. In the first place, the two roles (as well as the two domains) are identical. In the "is married to" relationship, the role on both sides is "spouse," just as the domain on both sides was "people." Thus we can no longer equate "degree" with the number of (distinct) roles. Also the "pattern" notion we used earlier doesn't fit quite as neatly. That was based on a concept of ordered pairs, where each position had some significance. Here we are really dealing with unordered pairs; the information is identically the same no matter which way the pieces are ordered. Saying that A and B are married is identically the same as saying that B and A are married. Few systems really support symmetric relationships; any that do are likely to require both pairs to occur, even though they are redundant.

Another difficulty is that the concept of "degree" is less clear. If the relationship is not limited to being between two people (and "sibling" isn't), then we can't really appeal to an intuitive notion of "pattern" to establish the notion of degree. The relationship might more naturally be viewed as one of varying degree, depending on the number of siblings in a given family. Nonetheless, we find it much more convenient to consider the relationships between people two at a time, and regularize this as a binary relationship.

ANTI-SYMMETRY

For some relationships, if X is related to Y, then Y cannot have the same relationship to X. Examples include "is manager of," "is parent of," and total orderings. ("Less than or equal" is a *partial* ordering, which permits some symmetries; "less than" is a *total* ordering, which is anti-symmetric.)

IMPLICATION (COMPOSITION)

A relationship may be defined as the composition of two others, i.e., the occurrence of two relationships implies a third. For example, if an employee works for a certain department and that department is in a certain division, then that employee belongs to that division. Or, one relationship may imply another: "is the husband of" implies an "is the wife of" relationship. The converse implication may or may not hold.

CONSISTENCY (SUBSET)

A certain kind of consistency between relationships might be obtained by defining one to be a subset of another. For example, the relationship between employees and their current departments is a subset of the relationship between employees and all their departments, as recorded in the personnel history file.

RESTRICTIONS

A variety of restrictions might be specified (cf. [Eswaran], [Hammer]). There may be a limit on the number of things that one thing can be related to (maximum department size). One relationship might require another to be true (an employee's manager must be in the same division, or must have a higher salary). It may be invalid to "close a path" (i.e., a part can't be a component of any of its sub-assemblies).

ATTRIBUTES AND RELATIONSHIPS OF RELATIONSHIPS

An instance of a relationship might have attributes of its own, such as when it was established (date of assignment to department). And it can itself be related to other things. This will come up again later.

> *The entity type Registration, for example, resolves the many-to-many relationship between Student and Class and contain its own attributes, such as Registration Date.*

NAMES

Relationships have names, and could be subject to the general variety of naming conventions.

The names of relationships comprise valid information. An information system should be able to answer questions like:

- What relationships exist between X and Y?
- In what relationships is X involved?

Naming Conventions

I tend to use one convention for naming relationships, but there are several others in use as well, and each of them seems to be more natural in certain cases. The conventions involve the use of zero, one, or two names for the relationship.

NO NAME

If we are speaking of an employee and mention "department," it can be recognized as a reference to the department to which the employee is assigned.

The convention is that, from a given entity, one traverses a relationship (selects a path) by naming the domain at the other end.

That works whenever (1) the relationship is binary, (2) the two domains are distinct, and (3) there is only one relationship between those two domains, or there is a convention for selecting one of them as a default.

This convention could be viewed as a degenerate form of the two-name convention (below), where each path has a name derived from the target domain. That is, "department of" is the name of the path from employee to department.

ONE NAME

The relationship may be given a single, neutral name such as "assignment" or "inventory." If we want to find a person's department, we ask about "assignment of person"; if we want to find the people in a department, we ask about "assignment of department."

This is a common convention, and one that I tend to use, but it doesn't correspond well with most of our language habits; we usually tend to use different words for the two directions of the relationship. Furthermore, if the two domains are the same, then the convention only works if the role names are mentioned. This convention could include the no-name case, if a defaulting mechanism were provided whenever the relationship name was omitted.

This convention is the one that extends best to n-ary relationships. Instead of getting involved with all the combinations of pairwise directions between the domains, one simply names the relationship and values in some set of domains, and expects as an answer all the combinations of values which exist with them in the other domains. For example, if a ternary relationship between parts, warehouses, and suppliers is given a single name such as INVENTORY, then questions can be written symmetrically using a form such as

```
INVENTORY (PART=PIN, WAREHOUSE=WEST, SUPPLIER=?)
```
or
```
INVENTORY (SUPPLIER=?, PART=?, WAREHOUSE=WEST)
```

TWO NAMES

A binary relationship can be traversed in two directions, and each is sometimes given its own name. (The two directions are sometimes described as two distinct paths.)

A hybrid between one and two names consists of the practice of giving the relationship one name, but requiring that it be modified in some way to indicate direction (e.g., by prefixing a minus sign for the direction considered to be "reverse").

This convention could eliminate the need for role names, but it does not extend well to n-ary relationships.

> *I typically show just one name (also known as a relationship label), capturing the business reason from parent entity to child entity. This is the more dominant*

business rule in a relationship and I show only this one name because almost all of the time, one can derive the name from the many entity to the one entity by reading the name on the one-to-many side. For example, here is how I would read the rules in the following model:

```
┌──────────────┐                         ┌──────────┐
│              │      contain            │          │
│   Machine    ├──○──────────────○<──────┤   Part   │
│              │                         │          │
└──────────────┘                         └──────────┘
```

- *Each Machine may contain one or many Parts.*
- *Each Part may be contained by one Machine.*

Notice how we can assume the relationship going the other way, in this case from Part back to Machine. Also, I read the relationship clockwise starting with the one side of the relationship, which addresses Kent's comment that in some way, we need to indicate direction. My labels also tend to be present tense verbs because we are really constructing sentences where the entity types on either end are nouns and the verb on the relationship connects the two entity types.

Relationships and Instances Are Entities

Instances of relationships are things themselves, about which we may have information in the system. They have attributes. Just as you have an age, so does your association with your department, your spouse, and your car. For a given part (type) stocked in a given warehouse, there is a certain quantity on hand.

They can be related to other things. The storing of a certain part in a certain warehouse is approved by a certain manager.

Instances of relationships can be related to each other (illustrated in Chapter 8).

Instances of a relationship can be identified (named) by identifying the relationship and the entities being related: "employed-in, John Jones, Accounting." In real systems these composite names of instances are usually not represented explicitly, but are implied by the definition and organization of the records in a file. A record in an employee file will explicitly contain "John Jones" and "Accounting"; "employed-in" is implicitly understood by users of the file, or may be factored out into a file or record description somewhere.

Steve's Takeaways

- Relationship labels must represent business reasons.

- Degree is the number of entity types that participate in a specific relationship.

- Referential integrity means that the data model can support the business assertions that are represented via relationships.

- Relationship characteristics include complexity, category constraints, self-relation, optionality, and number of forms.

- Subtyping is a popular modeling choice to help with integration.

- Recursion allows for flexibility but reduces model readability and obscures business rules.

Lots of things have lots of attributes. People have heights and birthdays and children, my car is blue, and New York is crowded. Much of the information in an information system records the attributes of things.

Some Ambiguities

But as common as the term "attribute" may be, I don't know what it means. The fact that I've been using the term is totally irrelevant.

The term is used to mean different things at different times, and I have trouble distinguishing the idea from others we've already discussed. Don't be fooled by the fact that I can rattle off a few examples. As you'll see later on, I really think they are examples of something else.

There are several ambiguities in the way the term is used. In order to explain that without getting tangled up in other ambiguities, let me temporarily introduce three new terms, so that we can get a better handle on what we're talking about. Every attribute has a *subject*: what it is an attribute of. People, my car, and New York were the subjects of the attributes in the examples above. Then there are *targets*, which are at the other end of the attribute, such as heights, blue, and crowded. Thirdly, there are *links* between subjects and targets. In the last example, it isn't "New York" or "crowded" which are important in themselves; what is being expressed is a connection between the two: New York *is* crowded.

(Later I'll show that the three new terms are quite imperfect. They still retain two ambiguities: type vs. instance, and thing vs. symbol.)

First ambiguity: "attribute" sometimes means the target, and sometimes the link. "Blue," "salary," "height" are sometimes referred to as attributes. On the other hand, "color of car" and "height of person" are also sometimes called attributes. If you don't make the distinction, you get trapped into believing that a single construct can represent the idea of "blue" and the set of all things that are blue. If you do make the distinction, then you had better use the term very carefully. About half the people you meet will use it in the opposite sense from you.

I tend to favor using the term "attribute" in the sense of the link itself, between the subject and the target. But I'm not sure I am always consistent in my usage (or that anyone else is).

> *I frequently use the term "data element" because "data elements" exist at both a logical and physical level of detail. Yet if I use the term "attribute," I need to remind myself to use a different term at the physical level, such as "column" or "field."*

The second ambiguity has to do with type and instance, and my new terms haven't helped that ambiguity one bit. Some people say that "blue" (or "my car is blue") is an attribute. Others will say that the attributes in this case are "color" (or "color of car"), and that the first two things were "values" (or instances, or occurrences) of the attribute. I have no preference. I tend to use the terms carelessly in either sense. Other people are sometimes careful to define the sense they intend, and sometimes they aren't.

> *The type vs. instance discussion is relevant for entities, relationships, and here, with attributes, as well.*

The third ambiguity has to do with thing and symbol, and my new terms didn't help in this respect either. When I explore some definitions of the target part of an attribute, I get the impression (which I can't verify from the definitions given!) that the authors are referring to the representations, e.g., the actual four letter sequence "b-l-u-e," or to the specific character sequence "6 feet." (Terms like "value," or "data item," occur in these definitions, without adequate further definition.) If I were to take that literally, then expressing my height as "72 inches" would be to express a different attribute from "six feet," since the "value" or "data item" is different. And a German describing my car as "blau," or a Frenchman calling it "bleu," would be expressing a different attribute from "my car is blue." Maybe the authors don't really mean that; maybe they really are willing to think of my height as the space between two points, to which many symbols might correspond as representations. But I can't be sure what they intend.

To summarize: any of the following might be an example fitting the concept of "attribute," although each exemplifies a different thing:

- The concept of color.
- The concept of blue.
- One of the character strings "blue," "bleu," "blau," etc.
- The general observation that cars have colors.
- The fact that my car is blue.

Perhaps these ambiguities can be resolved with some careful definitions, and some authors do make a commendable effort. Most definitional efforts I've seen, however, leave other crucial terms undefined or ambiguous, so that we don't really have a working basis for applying the concept.

> *Context is one of the common threads throughout this book. Earlier I shared that the admissions department at a university had a very different definition of Student than the alumni affairs department. Both departments are right in their definition of Student, it is only when we question the context, such as whether our scope is a particular department or the university as a whole, where issues frequently arise.*
>
> *Context also applies to Kent's discussion in this section. An automobile manufacturer most likely will have a stronger interest in vehicle color than a hotel. The manufacturer may, therefore, have a distinct entity containing the possible color set, whereas the hotel, who only needs a brief description of the car so they can locate the owner if needed, just needs the owner to write down the type of car and color; most likely one hotel guest writing "yellow orange" for their car and another hotel guest writing "orange yellow" will not cause an issue.*
>
> *Type vs. instance, symbol vs. words, attribute vs. relationship—these decisions can be made after understanding the proper context. In my book, **Data Modeling Made Simple, 2nd Edition**, Graeme Simsion contributed a chapter that I quote often on how the data modeler should work with other members of the project team. One of the key messages from this chapter is to always ask the higher questions. That is, upon seeing a model, instead of challenging the length of Customer Last Name or the spelling of Cost Center, ask questions such as, "What is the purpose of this data model?", "Who is the model for?", "What is the scope of the model?", etc. Questions such as these ensure the right context has been chosen.*

Attribute vs. Relationship

I'm really not very concerned about the ambiguities. For me, these problems are overshadowed by a larger concern. I don't know why we should define "attribute" as a separate construct at all. I can't tell the difference between attributes and relationships. (The astute reader may have noticed that I have, in two earlier comments, identified both attributes and relationships as constituting the bulk of the information managed in the system.)

> *Try to think of an attribute that cannot be modeled as a relationship, instead. Customer Last Name can be modeled as a relationship between a Customer and Name entity type. Order Date can be modeled as a relationship between an Order and Date entity type. The more important the concept that is being modeled, the greater the chance it will be a relationship and entity type instead of an attribute. Recall the context discussion from a few paragraphs ago. For example, the organization Esri created the ArcGIS Address Data Model, which models address information with such precision that many concepts we typically model as attributes are shown as relationships and entity types instead; to view this model, type in "ArcGIS Address Data Model" in any web search engine.*

The fact that "Henry Jones works in Accounting" has the same structure as the fact that "Henry Jones weighs 175 pounds." "175 pounds" appears to be the name of an entity in the category of "weights" just as much as "Accounting" is the name of an entity in the category of "departments." Both facts are relationships between entities. Both facts (relationships) are capable of themselves having attributes: Henry Jones has worked in Accounting since 1970; Henry Jones has weighed 175 pounds since 1970.

Both facts are answers to a symmetric set of questions:

- Where does Henry Jones work?
- How much does Henry Jones weigh?
- Who works in Accounting?
- Who weighs 175 pounds?

Both facts can be "traversed" in symmetric fashion to answer questions like:

- Who works in the same department as Henry Jones?
- Who has the same weight as Henry Jones?

Sundgren tries to make the distinction on the basis of whether the target is an object in the system—without defining what that means: "At any point of time every object in [the system] S possesses a set of properties. Some of the properties of an object are local, i.e., they are independent of the existence and properties of other objects in S. Other properties of an object are relational, i.e., they depend upon the object's relations to other objects in S" [Sundgren 74]. Then he confesses, in the ensuing discussion, that "...there are no formal criteria. However, I am convinced that useful informal rules of thumb can be given. Moreover, it is my experience that it is not a big problem for the user to make a satisfactory intuitive distinction between objects and properties."

> *Early in my career, I worked for a very skilled data modeler who, on my performance appraisal under areas for improvement, only had the phrase "Steve needs to feel the data more." It took me years to figure out exactly what the phrase meant. Sundgren uses the term "intuition" as my manager used the term "feel the data." Sometimes you just get a feel for what is right, and it is not always easy or possible to explain. The more you work in the data realm, the more you get a "feel" for how data should be categorized and described.*

Berild and Nachmens write: "We store information about objects...of two kinds, namely attributes of an object and an object's relations to other objects. Note that this distinction between attributes and relations is only of logical interest, as both attributes and relations are stored as associations..." [Berild].

There really does always seem to be an entity lurking behind the scenes somewhere, to which there separately corresponds an assortment of symbols exhibiting ambiguity and/or synonyms. We just have to learn to think of them properly. To accept the equivalence between attributes and relationships, we may have to acquire new habits of thought. My height really is not the string of characters "6 feet." A height (or other length) is a certain interval in space (any good reason not to think of it as an entity?); its measurement can be written down in many ways. A day is just that—a day on which you can think of something as having happened; there's a large assortment of ways to write the dates that are the names of that day. A color is something which you can see, and maybe has a definition in terms of light wave frequencies; it is not the word "blue."

Even with numbers, we have to distinguish between the abstract quantity and the various symbols that might represent it. When it comes to measured quantities, there are really two steps from entity to symbol:

1. From entity to abstract number, via a unit of measure. A unit of measure establishes relationships between mass entities and abstract numbers. The rule named "yards" maps my height into a number that is the same as the number of hands I have (which was mapped by a "count" relationship).
2. From abstract number to symbol, via data type, precision, base, notational system, etc. The symbol for my height in yards is "2" in decimal integers, "10" in binary integers, "II" in Roman numerals, and "two" in English words.

The target of an attribute is rarely a symbol directly. There is almost always a target entity distinct from the symbols. There are some notable exceptions to this rule, but then I wouldn't call the phenomenon an "attribute." If the target is really a pure symbol, then I prefer to call this "naming" and deal with it in another chapter. (It's confusing. Some people do prefer to say that name, employee number, and Social Security number are "attributes" of people. It's perfectly good jargon, but it does get some underlying distinctions muddled.)

In real practice, of course, dates, heights, managers, departments, etc. do get treated in diverse ways. But rather than classifying that in terms of attributes vs. relationships, I think it is more helpful to distinguish them on the basis of the kinds of existence (and equality) tests employed for the entities involved.

Incidentally, I do share with you the intuitive inclination to distinguish between relationships and attributes. For some facts the term "attribute" seems appropriate, and others seem to be "relationships." It's just that I can't find any really objective distinguishing criteria to support my intuitions consistently.

> ‖ *We need to get good at "feeling the data."*

Sometimes some of us might subconsciously picture it in terms of data records. If a fact is pictured just as a value in a field, we are inclined to call it an attribute, but if it has the effect of linking two records together, then it's a relationship. But that's an unsatisfactory basis for defining the distinction. First of all, we can conjure up many examples running counter to our intuitions. Secondly, the same fact can be represented inside the machine either way at various times. We want to define our basic information constructs in real world terms; the implementation in data processing mechanisms comes after we model the enterprise, not before.

Let me suggest a way to satisfy our intuitions. Let us build a modeling system that only supports one basic linking convention, which we are free to call either "attribute" or "relationship." The terms will be synonymous; we can use whichever one feels better at the moment.

If such a system doesn't satisfy you, I hope that you will tell me exactly what the system should do differently when it sees the terms "attribute" and "relationship."

Are Attributes Entities?

If one really wanted to develop a rigorous notion of attributes (which I don't), then this is another nasty question to be faced. Intuitively, some might say that attributes aren't themselves entities (regardless of whether one had in mind the links or the targets).

But if you think that relationships are entities, and you can't distinguish attributes from relationships, then where are you left?

And again: do you think that the subject of an attribute is necessarily an entity? I'm inclined to think so. But it turns out that some attributes are themselves the subjects of other attributes (which would make them entities after all). Examine carefully the structure of the following information, which is likely to be found in some databases:

- The percentage of an object's surface which is a given color.
- The date an employee began receiving a certain salary.
- The ages of an employee's children.

Those appear to be attributes of attributes.

And what about dates? They could have attributes, like day of week, or scheduled events. An illustration in [Sharman 75] shows a relation whose columns are month, day of month, and day of week.

Attribute vs. Category

We can say something *is* a car, and we can say that something *is* red. Intuitively, I feel that the first assertion is about the intrinsic nature of the thing (hence, its category), while the second asserts additional information about its characteristics (i.e., attributes). At one time I wanted to believe in a definable difference between category and attribute, but I didn't know how to articulate it. Some assertions fall in a middle ground ("that is an employee"), diminishing hopes for an effective distinction.

I've abandoned my hope of defining that distinction, too.

Options

In the area of attributes, just as with the other topics, we can apply the constructs to the data in a number of arbitrary ways, all of which make some sense to some people some time.

We can refine the structure of attributes to varying degrees. We tend to treat hair color as an attribute of a person, although a strict rendition perceives that color is an attribute of hair, which in turn is an entity related to a person. So also with date of hire, which is really the "starting time" attribute of the relationship between an employee and employer. We are often inconsistent, letting date of hire be an attribute of a person in the employee file, while treating it as the attribute of a relationship in the employment history file.

It sometimes makes sense to say that all colored things draw their attribute values from the same "domain." On the other hand, hair colors and car colors may not have many values in common. The list for the existence test may be different in the two cases!

A given set of things might be treated as the names of distinct fields (attributes?), or as the set of allowable values for a single field. We have all seen two kinds of forms for indicating, e.g., marital status. One has a heading "marital status," under which you are expected to fill in "married," "single," etc. The other kind has "married," "single," etc. as *headings* under which you are expected to make some mark (in this case the field values correspond to yes/no).

The same phenomenon might be an attribute, a categorization, or a relationship. Consider a person employed by a certain company:

- In a banking database in which companies are "non-entities," a person's employer is simply an attribute of the customer.
- In that company's database, that person falls in the category of "employees."
- In a more generalized database, "employed by" may be just one of several possible relationships between people and companies. Others might be "stockholder of," "sells to," "is covered by benefits of," etc.

> *Notice the common theme of defining the right context.*

And the view of the phenomenon will often change with time. That is, different perspectives become appropriate as the information processing needs of an enterprise change, and as the scope of interest changes.

Examples:

- If the databases of several companies are merged (e.g., for more efficient payroll processing), then the "employee" entity becomes a "person" entity with an explicit relationship to his company.
- Then, also, date of hire changes from an attribute of an employee to being an attribute of the relationship between person and company.
- When a company starts automating its personnel history records, the relationship between employee and department changes from 1:n to m:n.
- "Address" changes from a simple attribute to a complex one when residence histories are kept.
- Instead of address being an attribute of a person, it could become an attribute of a "place" entity. A "resides" relationship could be introduced between people and places.

- Some states generalize a driver's license into a general-purpose identification card. Then the attribute "is licensed to drive," which was implied for all cardholders in the old construct, now must be made an explicit attribute. Something similar probably happens when Social Security numbers are extended to serve as taxpayer identification numbers; it may no longer be true that a Social Security account exists for each of these numbers.

Conclusion

I will not formally distinguish between attributes and relationships, or between those two and categories. Even so, I do continue to use the terms "attribute" and "category" when they seem more natural, but I won't be able to say why they feel more natural at the time. Most likely, it will correlate well with my implicit assumptions about the existence tests for the entities involved.

Steve's Takeaways

- Every attribute has a *subject*: what it is an attribute of. Then there are *targets*, which are at the other end of the attribute. Thirdly, there are *links* between subjects and targets.

- Attributes have the same type vs. instance separation as entities and relationships.

- Type vs. instance, symbol vs. words, attribute vs. relationship—these decisions can be made after understanding the proper context. Always ask the higher questions to ensure proper context, such as, "What is the purpose of this data model?"

- The more important the concept being modeled is, the greater the chance it will be a relationship and entity type instead of an attribute.

- Experience as a data management professional usually leads to an ability to "feel the data."

- Symbols can speak louder than words. Height really is not the string of characters "6 feet." A height is a certain interval in space; its measurement can be written down in many ways. A day is just that—a day on which you can think of something as having happened. A color is something that you can see, and maybe has a definition in terms of light wave frequencies; it is not the word "blue." "Blue" represents the color.

Three ideas seem to have gotten combined:

- The urge to classify things according to "what they are."
- A need to express the semantic characteristics of things, by specifying which attributes and relationships and names are relevant and valid for them. The easiest paradigm: certain rules and constraints apply to certain *classes* of things.
- A tradition of data description, based on record types.

> *So, for example, an Account can be a Savings Account or a Checking Account. Kent's first point is that we would recognize both Savings and Checking Accounts as Accounts. His second point is that Savings Account may have distinct attributes and relationships from Checking Account, and vice versa. And his third point is that there is a tendency to "tag" both Checking Account as type Account and Savings Account as type Account.*

"Type": A Merging of Ideas

These often tend to be identified as the same phenomena. As a result, the concepts of "entity type" and "record type" are held to coincide. And they are often considered to represent a special kind of information, somehow distinct from other kinds.

> *This "special kind of information" is subtyping, where Account would be the supertype and Savings Account and Checking Account would be the two subtypes, as shown in this diagram:*

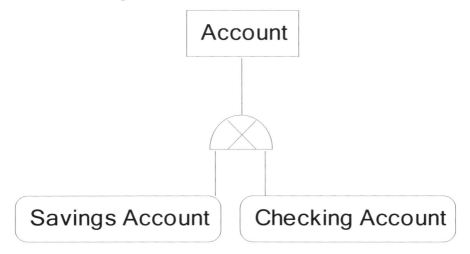

> *This model is read as, "Each Account can be either a Savings Account or a Checking Account. Each Savings Account is an Account. Each Checking Account is an Account." By the way, the concept of subtyping was created after the first edition of **Data and Reality** was written. Clive Finkelstein and James Martin created this concept in the 1980s based upon object-oriented programming techniques.[9]*

GUIDELINES

One common denominator is the notion of grouping. We assume that things can be divided into groups, where the groups are expected to satisfy a number of guidelines:

1. The groups correspond to our intuitive ideas of what things are, that is, classification.
2. The groups serve as the scopes over which naming conventions apply, that is, name syntaxes, uniqueness rules.
3. The groups serve as the scopes over which validity constraints apply.
4. The groups correspond to the domains of relationships.
5. Things don't move from one group to another.
6. The groups are mutually exclusive (nothing belongs to more than one such group)—an enormously bad hangover from the record type heritage, but still required in almost all definitions.

In any discussion of "type," it would be useful to establish which of these guidelines were to be assumed.

CONFLICTS

Unfortunately, these guidelines are generally quite incompatible.

As we've already seen, notions of "entity categorization" are very variable, subjective, and dependent on local purpose. We have "categories" for which naming conventions aren't uniformly applicable, for which attributes aren't universally applicable.

Some people don't have Social Security numbers; some don't have maiden names. If a category is defined to be the union of several sub-categories, a rule for one sub-category may not apply to another. Further, we may not want to formally define sub-categories corresponding to the scope of every rule, e.g., just for married female employees.

---

[9] Read the article "Graphics—Data Modeling" from www.informit.com for more on data modeling history.

Books may have International Standard Book Numbers (ISBN) and Library of Congress numbers. Some books have both, some have neither, some have one or the other. The category of things covered by Library of Congress numbers includes photographs, movies, tapes, recordings, etc. Those don't get ISBNs.

> *A Global Trade Item Number (GTIN) is a globally unique identifier to ensure each product, including books, photographs, movies, tapes, recordings, etc., has one unique ID. Many existing identifiers such as the ISBN fit within the GTIN structure. However, even with this global way of identifying products, we still run into problems. For example, many book publishers use the same ISBN for both a print book and an ebook, which are two different mediums and therefore two different products that should really have two distinct ISBNs.*

Record types are probably the only concept to which the guideline of being mutually exclusive is applicable.

> *This is because the data modeler can make up identifiers such as counters.*

I would speculate that for each pair of guidelines in the list above, we could find some example that brought the two into conflict.

Extended Concepts

ARBITRARY SETS

Consider arbitrary groupings: sets defined in terms of things satisfying certain predicates, e.g., having certain relationships to certain things, or Boolean combinations of such conditions. Such conditions could be based on attribute values, relationships to other things, names, etc. It's not clear why "type" is a different idea from these, or which of these is to be thought of as "type." There are some good reasons not to make type quite so distinct.

For example, there should be some way to present categories as properties (e.g., field values) to applications. That is, if someone is both an employee and a stockholder, then

- An application dealing with stockholder records should be able to see employer name as a field value, and
- An application dealing with employee records should be able to see a field indicating stockholder status.

Conversely, properties may be used to define "apparent" categories to applications, probably as subsets of "real" categories. For example, a new application may want to deal with a file of managers (perhaps with department records also occurring in the file). "Manager" appears to be the category (i.e., file name or record type) to the application, but it is defined to the system as that subset of the "employees" category which has "manager" as the value of the "job" attribute.

> *It is a very interesting distinction between type and group. I have found that types are reserved for more standardized and recognized ways of categorizing things, whereas groups tend to be more customized and defined on an ad hoc, as-needed basis. For example, a type might allow us to categorize products by brand. This categorization most likely is determined at a corporate level within an organization. A grouping, however, might involve viewing all frozen products as a category to ensure transportation containers have the required refrigeration, which is more of a localized requirement that is perhaps only of use to the shipping department.*

GENERAL CONSTRAINTS

We haven't lost sight of the original objective, namely to be able to specify rules about "groups" of things. But now the groups need not be so explicit; we can speak in terms of how we'll recognize the individuals to which the rules apply. Rules and constraints can be generalized to the form, "The following rule applies to all things satisfying a certain predicate," where the predicate might be "all things having relationship X to object Y."

For traditionalists, X might be "has type" and Y could be "employee." For set theorists, X would be "is member" and Y would be "employees." For others, X might be "is employed" and Y might be "IBM."

It is thus a matter of viewpoint as to whether the fundamental constructs involved here are sets and membership or entities and relationships.

This general form solves the "partial applicability" problem: we can specify that "maiden name" is applicable to all things which are employees of IBM and which are of the female gender and which have been married.

Some of the rules might govern the interaction of the sets themselves: two sets may not overlap (equivalently: if one relationship holds for a given entity then another relationship can't, and vice versa); one set may be a subset of another (the defining relationship of one implies the other); and so on.

In making types non-exclusive, we come closer to reality—and suffer the penalty of facing more of the complexities of real life. We now have to deal with the interaction of rules that apply to overlapping sets. Sometimes they can get inconsistent: employees might be required to do something stockholders are forbidden to do. It would take some complex analysis to insure that a large set of specified constraints was entirely consistent. But saying that this is a disadvantage of overlapping types is the view of the ostrich. Exclusive sets don't solve the problem; they avoid it by pretending that employees and stockholders don't overlap.

> *Exclusive (also known as non-overlapping) subtyping means that a supertype can be any one of its subtypes, but not more than one at a time. Inclusive (non-exclusive), also known as overlapping subtyping means that a supertype can be more than one of its subtypes at the same time. In the two models below, the exclusion version would mean that an Account can be either a Savings Account or a Checking Account, but not both. The non-exclusive or overlapping version would allow an Account to be both a Savings and a Checking Account.*

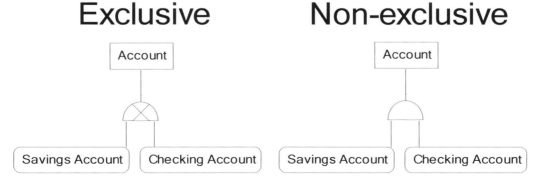

Problems of overlap and consistency can even occur with respect to specifying existence and equality tests. This can arise when there is an overlap of "types," where some members have explicit surrogates and some don't. Consider a personnel database that has explicit surrogates (records) for employees, but not for dependents. This is fine so long as we are willing to treat employees and dependents as disjoint categories. But suppose we needed to know which dependents are also employees? Dependents are usually listed by name only, and that is not an unambiguous key to the employee file. An employee might have the same name as someone else's dependent (or his own son!). Various solutions can be devised, none of them elegant.

The same situation can occur in a banking database, in which a client's employer might be a simple attribute (field value). The bank may want to be able to determine whether a client's employer was itself a client of the bank.

TYPES, IF YOU WANT THEM

Given a general mechanism for describing sets, one can try to superimpose a notion of "type" by imposing rules such as these:

- Some sets confer naming rules on their members.
- Every object must "belong" to at least one such set (which means that the object has the required relationships to appropriate objects).
- Once a member of such a set, the object may not leave the set, except when the object is deleted from the system.
- Such sets could be called "types," but underneath it all they are still ordinary sets.

If that doesn't satisfy your notion of type, just vary the rules to suit yourself. Then compare notes with your neighbor.

Sets

Be cautious in equating sets with attributes (this bears on the ambiguities mentioned in Chapter 5). For example, we might have an object representing the set of employees in the aggregate, and an object representing the concept of "employee"—and then be tempted to say they are the same object. We might have observed apparent redundancies. Certain patterns of relationships occur in parallel with the two objects: a person has the attribute of being an "employee" if and only if he is a member of the set of employees. So why keep them apart?

SETS AND ATTRIBUTES

The difficulty is that the concept of "employee" determines more than one set. The set I had in mind consisted of people who are currently employees. (That's what you had in mind too, isn't it?) But people can be related to the concept in many ways. There are people who have been employees, or are eligible to become, or have applied to be, or have pretended to be, or refused to be, and so on, together with various combinations of these sets which yield new sets. For other kinds of concepts, other relationships might also be relevant, such as "partly," or "almost," or "occasionally."

> *Often what causes a thing to belong to more than one set, or to change sets, is lifecycle. A person who is eligible to become an employee may belong to a different set than a person who has retired from being an employee. Both job applicants and retired employees are different sets of employees and represent two of the numerous lifecycles an employee can travel through.*

A set is determined by a predicate, whose minimal form involves a relationship to an object: the set of things having relationship X to object Y. One should not presume that the object Y determines a single set.

TYPE VS. POPULATION (INTENSION VS. EXTENSION)

A "type" is sometimes referred to as a set of occurrences (e.g., the type "employee" consists of the set of employees). This is all right as an informal concept, but several precautions ought to be observed [Durchholz].

There are two distinct notions of "set" involved here. There is the abstract idea of what the type is (e.g., the idea of "employee"), and the current population of people who happen to be employees at the moment. The former is the "intension" of the set, and the latter is its "extension." The latter tends to change often (as people get hired and fired), but the former doesn't.

Very simply, a "type" corresponds to the intension of a set, not its extension. The concept of "employee" isn't altered by hiring and firing people.

Incidentally, one ought to be very cautious about claims of various models being based on "the axioms of traditional set theory." That set theory deals entirely with extensional sets: a set is determined entirely by its population. There is simply no notion of a set with changing population; each different population constitutes a different set. So, the relevance of such set theory to any model of data processing is, at the very least, questionable.

Another caution has to do with emptiness. The concept of "employee" continues to exist even if there are no employees. One oughtn't think that the concept has disappeared just because no space is occupied by employee records.

Again, this simply amounts to distinguishing the intension and extension of the set. And, to those familiar with set theory, it corresponds to the existence of an empty set (i.e., the set, though empty, does itself exist).

As a consequence of its extensional foundation, traditional set theory holds that there is exactly one empty set. In fact, this provides the set theoretic base for number theory: the empty set is the definition of the concept of "one."

> *Recall the concept of "null." Null means empty, but in tagging something as empty, we recognize that "empty" is a value and therefore not really empty. This is why many people (and even software tools) get confused by nulls.*

Thus, if all employees are fired, then the set of employees is the same as the set of unicorns. Not two equivalent sets, but one single solitary set to which we may give several names. Again, this doesn't correspond to our data processing models: "employee" and "unicorn" are always two distinct types, or concepts.

This distinction between extension and intension affirms that a type (set) is a distinct entity from any of its members. One could perceive set membership, or type membership, in terms of a relationship between pairs of entities: set objects and member objects.

REPRESENTATION OF SETS

Sets need not be introduced as primitive kinds of objects. They can be generalized into objects and relationships. "Belonging" can be a relationship between an arbitrary object and an object representing a set; "subset" can be a relationship between two objects representing sets. With a strong enough capability for implication and constraint on relationships (see Chapter 4), the behavior of sets can be modeled. That is, we can specify a derived relationship: X "belonging" to Y and Y being "subset" of Z generates X "belonging" to Z.

Thus, the basic mechanism of objects and relationships seems adequate to cover the phenomena of types and sets. It's useful, too, because types and sets share many of the characteristics of common objects. They have names (and perhaps aliases), and attributes (creation date, number of members), and relationships with other things: they are subsets of one another, people are responsible for maintaining them, they are governed by constraints, etc.

Steve's Takeaways

- Three ideas overlap: 1) The urge to classify things according to "what they are," so we would recognize both Savings and Checking Accounts as Accounts. 2) A need to express the semantic characteristics of things, so a Savings Account may have distinct attributes and relationships from a Checking Account, and vice versa. 3) A tradition of data description, based on record types, so there is a tendency to "tag" Checking Account as type Account and Savings Account as type Account.

- Subtyping is a useful way to merge ideas. Clive Finkelstein and James Martin created this concept in the 1980s based upon object-oriented programming techniques.

- Record types are probably the only concept to which the guideline of being mutually exclusive is applicable, because the data modeler can make identifiers up.

- It is not always clear how to distinguish types and groups. I reserve types for more standardized and recognized ways of categorizing things, whereas groups are for more customized and ad hoc ways of categorizing things.

- Exclusive, also known as non-overlapping, subtyping means that a supertype can be any one of its subtypes, but not more than one at a time. Inclusive, also known as overlapping, subtyping means that a supertype can be more than one of its subtypes at the same time. In reality, most subtypes are overlapping.

- Often what causes a thing to belong to more than one set, or to change sets, is lifecycle.

- This distinction between extension and intension affirms that a type (set) is a distinct entity from any of its members.

We return now to the domain of computerized information systems. The bridge that gets us back is the "data model." It is a bridge in the sense that data models are techniques for representing information, and are at the same time sufficiently structured and simplistic as to fit well into computer technology.

> *I distinguish "data modeling" from "data model." Data modeling is the process of eliciting business requirements and organizing the data to produce a data model. The data model becomes the artifact that can be used and reused to avoid performing the same data modeling activities again and again.*

General Concept of Models

We are always in trouble with words. The term "model" is so overused as to be absurd. Out of the whole complex of meanings it might have, the following is what I have in mind at the moment.

A model is a basic system of constructs used in describing reality. It reflects a person's deepest assumptions regarding the elementary essence of things. It may be called a "world view." It provides the building blocks, the vocabulary that pervades all of a person's descriptions. In the broad arena of human thought, some alternative models might be composed of physical objects and motion, or of events seen statically in a time-space continuum, or of the interactions of mystical or spiritual forces, and so on.

> *I define a data model as a set of symbols and text that describe some information landscape. The data model is a wayfinding tool that helps developers and analysts better understand a set of attributes and business rules.*

A model is more than a passive medium for recording our view of reality. It shapes that view, and limits our perceptions. If a mind is committed to a certain model, then it will perform amazing feats of distortion to see things structured that way, and it will simply be blind to the things which don't fit that structure.

Some linguists have been telling us that for a while. "...[L]anguage defines experience for us...because of our unconscious projection of its implicit expectations into the field of experience.... Categories such as number, gender, case, tense, mode, voice, aspect, and a host of others...are not so much discovered in experience as imposed upon it" [Sapir].

In much narrower terms, the data processing community has evolved a number of models in which to express descriptions of reality. These models are highly structured, rigid, and simplistic, being amenable to economic processing by computer. These models include such things as files of records, tabular structures, graphs (networks) of lines connecting points, hierarchies (tree structures), and sets.

Some members of that community have been so overwhelmed by the success of a certain technology for processing data that they have confused this technology with the natural semantics of information. They have forgotten any other way to think of information except as regimented hordes of rigidly structured data codes—in short, the mentality of the punched card.

> *Not only have I seen technology constraining the thoughts of information technology professionals, but I also frequently see this artificial view of the world adopted by some business professionals. For example, when I interview users, trying to determine "what they do," they often phrase how their business works in terms of the technology they use. For example, "First I enter an order in this system, then this system tells me if the product exists in inventory...." Recall the tainted-thinking commentary I shared in Kent's 1978 preface.*

The Logical Model: Sooner, or Later?

All the problems touched on in this book converge on the logical model (see Chapter 2). It is in this medium that all the things an enterprise deals with must be reduced to crisply structured descriptions.

The logical model will be a very real computer-related construct, just like a program or a data file. An enterprise is going to have a large amount of time, effort, and money invested in the logical model.

There is the learning investment. In spite of our best efforts, any formalism we adopt as the basis of the logical model will still be an artificial structure. The concepts will not be perfectly intuitive to anyone; the rules, limitations, and idiosyncrasies will have to be learned. There will be a formal language to be learned, as well as operating procedures. (Interactive facilities and other design aids may help—after the bugs get ironed out— but even their use has to be learned.)

> *The modeling tools today are much better than they were in 1978.*

Then comes the actual modeling effort. A lot of energy will go into forcing a fit between the model and the enterprise. The correspondences won't always be obvious; there will be lots of alternatives, and it will take some iterations to recognize the best choices.

Sometimes it will take a flash of insight to perceive the real world in a new way, which better fits the model. Sometimes the enterprise itself will be altered to fit the model. (It's not unusual for a company to adopt a whole new part numbering scheme before automating their inventory control.) This is all accompanied by the gargantuan task of simply collecting and coordinating a mountainous heap of descriptions.

> *Looking at the same information landscape through the eyes of a particular project, and then through the eyes of the enterprise, often produces two very different pictures. Recall how important context is from earlier discussions.*

"Many corporations will be carrying out the lengthy job over the next 10 years of defining the thousands of data-item types they use and constructing, step by step, suitable schemas from which their databases will be built. The description of this large quantity of data will be an arduous task involving much argument between different interested parties. Eventually the massive databases that develop will become one of the corporation's major assets" [Martin].

> *Are we there yet? James Martin wrote this in 1975. I believe most companies are still far from completing this comprehensive and high quality type of mapping.*

The end result will be a physically large volume of information. "It must be emphasized...that the logical schema is a real and tangible item made most explicit in machine readable form, couched in some well defined and potentially standardizable language" [ANSI]. Think of it in the same orders of magnitude as a program library, or a system catalog, or a payroll file. Think of cylinders of disk space, and printouts many inches thick. Think of a small army of technical personnel who have been indoctrinated in a particular way of conceptualizing data, and who have mastered the intricacies of a new language and the attendant operational procedures.

All this time, manpower, and money will be invested by customers in any logical model supported in a major system. We had better be very careful about the architecture of the first one. Any attempt to replace it with a better one later will threaten that investment; customers won't accept the replacement any faster than they now accept a major new programming language, or a new operating system. And the replacements will forever be hamstrung by compatibility and migration requirements.

> *So it is a very good idea to get the logical data model right the first time!*

Unfortunately, there are some natural forces which work against our getting it right the first time.

We are just entering a transitional phase in data description. The idea of having three levels of data description (i.e., including a logical model) has been much researched and written about ([ANSI], [GUIDE-SHARE]), but it hasn't yet taken serious hold in any significant commercial systems. It's still on the horizon; it's an idea whose time is just about to come. (I hope I won't still be saying that ten years from now.)

> *I think we are still saying this! Many organizations have accurate physical data models, but are missing conceptual and logical data models, or have conceptual and logical data models that are inferior to or out-of-date as compared to their physical data model counterparts.*

The builders and users of today's commercial systems quite justifiably want to avoid cluttering their systems with anything that might impair efficiency and productivity. The argument that this new approach will make the overall management of data more productive in the long run has yet to be convincingly demonstrated to them.

> *On many Agile development projects today, for example, the idea of a Big Design Up Front (BDUF) is frowned upon as an activity that slows down delivery of the actual system.*

The need for a more sophisticated descriptive model will only gradually achieve general recognition. It will come from the headaches of trying to crunch together the diverse record formats and data structures used by growing families of applications operating on the same integrated database. The nonsense of trying to reflect all their record formats in the logical model, while still pretending that the logical model describes the entities of the enterprise, will become apparent.

The need for a more sophisticated approach to data description will also grow as the interfaces of the data systems expand to involve more people who are not trained in computer disciplines. Such people will be involved both as end users and as managers of the information resource. Someday there will be a general recognition of what it means, and what it's worth, to model entities and relationships instead of data items and records. I hope that recognition won't come too late.

> *Are we there yet? We are still "fighting the fight," expending a lot of effort to convince the business of the need for and value of the logical data model.*

Models of Reality vs. Models of Data

One thing we ought to have clear in our minds at the outset of a modeling endeavor is whether we are intent on describing a portion of "reality" (some human enterprise), or a data processing activity.

> *Great discussion of this topic in* **Data Modeling Theory and Practice,** *by Graeme Simsion. That is, is data modeling really "design" or something different?*

Most models describe data processing activities, not human enterprises.

They pretend to describe entity types, but the vocabulary is from data processing: fields, data items, values. Naming rules don't reflect the conventions we use for naming people and things; they reflect instead techniques for locating records in files (cf. [Stamper 77]).

Failure to make the distinction leads to confusion regarding the roles of symbols in the representation of entities, and some mixed ideas of "domain."

Steve's Takeaways

- The data model is a bridge for representing information, and at the same time sufficiently structured and simplistic as to fit well into computer technology.

- "Data modeling" is the process of eliciting business requirements and organizing the data to produce a "data model." The data model becomes the artifact that can be used and reused to avoid performing the same data modeling activities again and again.

- A model is a basic system of constructs used in describing reality. It reflects a person's deepest assumptions regarding the elementary essence of things.

- Some information technology professionals have been so overwhelmed by the success of a certain technology for processing data that they have confused this technology with the natural semantics of information.

- Looking at the same information landscape through the eyes of a particular project, and then through the eyes of the enterprise, often produces two very different pictures.

- The 1975 dream of having all attributes understood and "mapped" is still not a reality for most organizations.

Records provide a very efficient basis for processing data. They enable us to map out very regular storage structures. They make it easy to write iterative programs for processing large volumes of data. They make it easy to partition data into convenient units for moving around, locking up, creating, destroying, etc.

In short, record technology reflects our attempt to find efficient ways to process data. It does not reflect the natural structure of information. Senko refers to "a major commitment to particular restrictive representations like the arrays of scientific computation, the extensional aspects of set notations, the n-tuples of relations, the cards, records, files, or data sets of commercial systems and the static categories of natural language grammars. Each of these representations has great merit for its original area of study, and in turn it has made major contributions to the study of information systems. Nonetheless, each provides only an approximate fit to the evolving, heterogeneous, interconnected information structures required to model real world enterprises" [Senko 75b]. Sowa observes: "Historically, database systems evolved as generalized access methods. They addressed the narrow issue of enabling independent programs to cooperate in accessing the same data. As a result, most database systems emphasize the questions of how data may be stored or accessed, but they ignore the questions of what the data means to the people who use it or how it relates to the overall operations of a business enterprise" [Sowa 76].

Record technology is such an ingrained habit of thought that most of us fail to see the limitations it forces on us. It didn't matter much in the past, because our real business was record processing almost by definition. But we want to approach the logical model a little differently. We want it to reflect information, rather than data processing technology. When different applications deal with the same information using different record technologies, those differences shouldn't clutter up the logical model. (And we might want to consider the possibility of future data technologies that are not so record oriented.)

> *The logical data model is so valuable because it is technology-independent, and therefore can be used many times as a starting point for multiple physical data models. Even with technologies that are not relational such as NoSQL databases, the logical data model still applies.*

When I use the term "record," I have in mind a fixed linear sequence of field values, conforming to a static description contained in catalogs and in programs. A record description consists largely of a sequence of field descriptions, each specifying a field name, length, and data type. Each such record description determines one record type.

One field (sometimes a combination of several fields) is often designated as the key, whose values uniquely distinguish and identify occurrences of this type of record.

As far as the system is concerned, a field name signifies a space in the record occupied by data in a certain representation. Any other semantic significance of the field name is perceived only by the user.

Some record formats allow a certain variability by permitting a named field or group of fields to occur a variable number of times within a record (i.e., as a list of values or sets of values). I will use the term *normalized system* to refer to systems that do not permit repeating groups or fields. This follows from the relational model, which excludes such repetitions via its normalization requirements (specifically, first normal form; [Codd 70], [Kent 73]).

> *First normal form (1NF) requires that all attributes on the model contain only a single piece of business information, and that the same attribute can appear once, at most, in an entity. For example, in the two models on the facing page, the one on the left is not in 1NF. This is because there are three phone numbers, so the 'same' attribute appears three times. Also, Customer Name contains both the first and last name of the customer, so Customer Name includes two pieces of information instead of just a single piece. The model on the right is in 1NF because the phone numbers have been separated into their own table, and Customer First Name and Customer Last Name appear as two separate attributes.*

Not in 1NF

Customer

Customer Number
Customer Name Customer Phone Number 1 Customer Phone Number 2 Customer Phone Number 3

In 1NF

Customer

Customer Number
Customer First Name Customer Last Name

be reached at

Customer Phone

Customer Number (FK) Phone Type Code (FK)
Customer Phone Number

categorize

Phone Type

Phone Type Code
Phone Type Name

Semantic Implications

Much of the meaning of a record is supplied by the mind of the user, who intuits many real world implications that "naturally" follow from the data. Quite often these implications are buried in the procedures encoded in specific application programs written to process the records. But if we strip away such inferred interpretations, and look only at the semantics that inherently reside in the record construct, we find the following presumptions about the nature of information:

- Any thing has exactly one type—because a record has exactly one record type. We are not prepared for multiple answers to "What kind of thing is that?"
- All things of the same type have exactly the same naming conventions and the same kinds of attributes—because all records of the same type have the same fields.

- The kinds of names and attributes applicable to an entity are always predictable and don't change much—because our systems presume stable record descriptions in the catalog or dictionary, and because we've learned that it's traumatic to reformat a file of records.

- There is a natural and necessary distinction between data and data descriptions. We are accustomed to having record descriptions in catalogs, and in programs, quite separate and different from data files.

- In particular, the name of the relationship occurring between two entities is not information, since it doesn't occur in the data file. For that matter, neither does the type of an entity (i.e., the contents of a record don't tell us that the thing represented in a certain field is an "employee").

- A record, being the unit of creation and destruction, naturally represents one entity. Anything not represented by a record is not an entity.

- Such entities are the only things about which we have data. The key field of a record identifies one such entity; all other fields provide information about that entity, and not about any other entity. (This is the fundamental information structure implied by the format of a single record.)

- All entities have unique identifiers. Or at the very least, all entities are distinguishable from each other. That is, for any two entities, we must know some fact that is different about them, which we can use to tell them apart.

- Each kind of fact about an entity always involves entities (or attribute values) of a single type. We don't expect two different kinds of entities to occur in the "employer" fields of two people's records; the record system doesn't have any way of telling us which type is occurring in that field for a particular record occurrence.

- And the entities or attribute values involved in a given kind of fact all have the same form of name (representation). We don't have self-describing records which tell us which data type or format is being used in this particular record occurrence.

- A given entity should be referenced by the same name (representation) everywhere it occurs. The only way we know if two references are to the same thing is by a match on the fields containing those references.

- There is an essential difference between entities and attribute values, and between relationships and attributes. The difference seems to correlate with the things that are or aren't represented by records. If there's a record, then the thing it represents is an entity, and a reference to it in a field comprises a relationship (as in the department field of an employee record). But if there is no separate record for the thing, then a reference to it involves neither an entity nor a relationship; it's simply an attribute value (as in the salary or spouse fields of an employee record).

- Relationships are not distinct constructs to be represented in a uniform way. Obviously; otherwise we wouldn't be provided with so confusingly many ways to represent them.

- Many-to-many relationships are (usually) entities in their own right. And the associations implied by multi-valued attributes are also entities, even though they aren't relationships. (This all follows from their being represented by distinct records.) But one-to-many relationships are (usually) not entities.

- Relationships and compound identifiers are the same phenomenon, since they can have the same representation.

The Type/Instance Dichotomy

The dichotomy between types itself makes some limiting presumptions about information.

AN INSTANCE OF EXACTLY ONE TYPE

If we intend to use a record to represent a real world entity, there is some difficulty in equating record types with entity types. It seems reasonable to view a certain person as a single entity (for whom we might wish to have a single record in an integrated database). But such an entity might be an instance of several entity types, such as employee, dependent, customer, stockholder, etc. It is difficult, within the current record processing technologies, to define a record type corresponding to each of these, and then permit a single record to simultaneously be an occurrence of several of the record types.

Note that we are not dealing with a simple nesting of types and subtypes: all employees are people, but some customers and stockholders are not.

To fit comfortably into a record-based discipline, we are forced to model our entity types as though they did not overlap. We are required to do such things as thinking of customers and employees as always distinct entities, sometimes related by an "is the same person" relationship. At most, it might be possible to model a simple type and subtype structure, where records of the subtype can be obtained by simply eliminating irrelevant fields from the containing type.

DESCRIPTIONS ARE NOT INFORMATION

The information in a file consists mainly of field values occurring in records. Thus there is likely to be a data item answering the question, "Who manages the Accounting department?" The manager's name can be found in a field somewhere. But it is not likely that the file can provide an answer to "How is Henry Jones related to the

Accounting department?" There are no fields in the file containing such entries as "is assigned to," "was assigned to," "on loan to," "manages," "audits," "handles personnel matters for," etc. Depending on how the records are organized, the answer generally consists of a field name or a record type name, which are not contained in the database. To a naïve seeker of information from the database, it is not at all obvious why one question may be asked and the other may not.

It's not just that he can't get an answer; the interfaces don't provide any way to frame the question. The data management systems do not provide a way to ask such questions whose answers are field names or record type names.

Then consider the following questions:
1. How many employees are there in the Accounting department?
2. What is the average number of employees per department?
3. What is the maximum number of employees currently in any department?
4. What is the maximum number of employees permitted in any department?
5. How many more employees can be hired into the Accounting department?

If the maximum number of employees permitted is fixed by corporate policy, then a system offering advanced validation capabilities is likely to place that number into a constraint in a database description, outside the database itself. Our naïve seeker of facts will then again find himself unable to ask the last two questions. He might well observe that other things having the effect of rules or constraints are accessible from the database, such as sales quotas, departmental budgets, head counts, safety standards, etc. The only difference, which doesn't matter much to him, is that some such limits are intended to be enforced by the system, while others are not.

This suggests that we might want to seek a way to represent such constraints in the same format—and in the same database—as "ordinary" information, but with the added characteristic that they are intended to be executed and enforced by the data processing system.

It is true that descriptions and constraints are inherently different from other data with respect to their update characteristics. Changes to these imply differences in the system's behavior, ranging from changes in validation procedures to physical file reorganizations implied by format changes. But such descriptions and constraints need not be inherently different for retrieval purposes. And even with respect to updating, the method need not be inherently different as perceived by users. It is only necessary that the authorization to do so be carefully controlled, and that the consequences be propagated into the system.

REGULARITY (HOMOGENEITY)

Record structures work best when there is a uniformity of characteristics over the population of an entity type. It is usually necessary for the entire population to be subject to the same naming conventions (e.g., there has to be something that can serve as a key field over the entire population). It is usually assumed that all instances of the entity type are eligible to participate in the same relationships.

Most fundamentally, it is presumed that the entire population has the same kinds of attributes. While exceptions are tolerated, the essential configuration is that of a homogeneous population of records, all having the same fields. The underlying assumption is that field names can be factored out of the data.

The more we deviate from this norm of homogeneity, the less appropriate is the record configuration. There are certain techniques for accommodating variability among instances in a record structure, but these need to be used sparingly. If there can be considerable variation among entity instances, then the solutions become cumbersome and inefficient. Such solutions include:

- Define the record format to include the union of all relevant fields, where not all the fields are expected to have values in every record. Thus many records might have null values in many fields.
- Define the *same* field to have different meanings in different records. Unfortunately, such a practice is never defined to the system. With respect to any processing done by the system, that field appears to have the same significance in every record occurrence. It certainly has only one field name, which in these cases usually turns out to be something totally innocuous and uninformative, like CODE or FIELD1. It is only the buried logic in application programs which knows the significance of these fields, and the different meanings they have in different records.

Many entity types come to mind for which considerable variability of attributes is likely to occur, such as people, tools, clothing, furniture, vehicles, etc. For example, in a file of clothing records, consider which of the following field names are relevant (and what they might mean) in each record: size, waist size, neck size, sleeve length, long or short sleeves, cup size, inseam length, button or zipper, gender, fabric type, heel size, width, color, pattern, pieces, season, number, collar style, cuffs, neckline, sleeve style, weight, flared, belt, waterproof, formal or casual, age, pockets, sport, washable....

You can play the same game with the other entity types, or even try to extend this list.

I agree with Kent that the two solutions given for accommodating different record configurations within the same entity type produces a suboptimal solution. Defining the record format to include the union of all relevant fields leads to structures that are incredibly difficult to analyze. Defining the same field to have different meanings in different records, although frequently done in packaged software under the guise of such as names as User Customized Field 1, Miscellaneous Field 25, etc., leads to a lot of work later on to figure out what those fields really mean.

There are at least two better ways of modeling entity types whose instances require different attributes, and I'll illustrate both using the Clothing entity type example that Kent provided several paragraphs back.

One option is to keep all of the common attributes in the main entity type and use generic domain entities to accommodate all of the extra data elements, as shown in this example:

The entity type Clothes would contain all of the common attributes, with only three being shown in this example. We can easily handle Heel Size because it is an entity instance in the Clothes Quantity entity for each Clothes entity instance that needs the Heel Size attribute. The attribute Clothes Quantity Description would contain the value "Heel Size" so that we do not lose the attribute name. Zipper Indicator would be defined once in Clothes Indicator Type and each Clothes entity instance that needs this attribute would have a value in Clothes Indicator. Likewise, Pattern Name would be populated once in Clothes Name Type and then referenced for each Clothes entity instance that has a pattern.

The other option is to use subtyping by putting all of the common attributes in the supertype and the attributes specific to a given subtype in their appropriate subtype. So returning to the clothing example, we can put "Heel Size" in the Shoe subtype, Pattern Name in the Shirt subtype, and Zipper Indicator in the Pants subtype. Please refer to the following diagram.

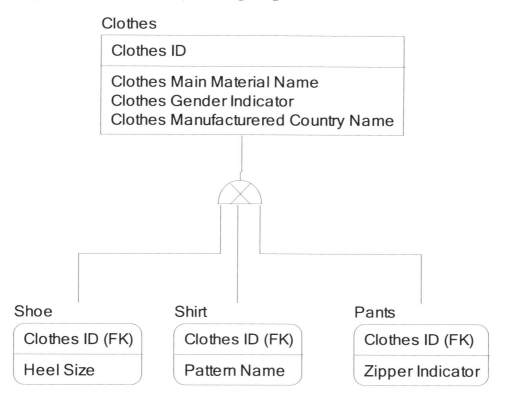

Naming Practices

Record structures work best when there is an exact one-to-one correspondence between entities and their names (representations), i.e., no synonyms or ambiguities. And they work best when all entities of a given type have the same name formats (representation). Under these conditions, it is feasible to have a single format specified for a field in which these entities might occur. And it is easy to detect references to the same entity: just match the contents of the fields.

Real entities don't always behave so simply. The employees of a multinational corporation might not all have Social Security numbers, or employee numbers (or they might be in different formats in different countries). But many employees have both, and some may have several Social Security numbers. Some books don't have International Standard Book Numbers (ISBN), others don't have Library of Congress numbers, and some have neither. But many books have both—and some have several ISBNs. And Library of Congress numbers apply to a larger class of entities than do ISBNs; they are also assigned to films, recordings, and other forms of publication, in addition to books. Oil companies have their own conventions for naming their own oil wells, and the American Petroleum Institute has also assigned "standard" names to some wells—but not all.

For all practical purposes, record systems can't cope with partially applicable names. In order to use records for an application, it is necessary that some naming convention be adopted which applies to all occurrences of the entity type.

Synonyms are not really managed at all, as far as the structure and description of data are concerned. If fields in two different record types contain employee numbers, then the system can perceive that some of these records might refer to the same person. (This is, in fact, the fundamental mechanism for expressing relationships in the relational model—matching field values imply that two records are related, and can be "joined.") But if one record type contains Social Security numbers instead, then this knowledge is lost. As far as the system is concerned, there are no potential relationships here. It is only in the minds of users, and in procedural logic buried in programs, that any suspicion lurks that these might in fact refer to the same people.

And in all of this, we haven't bothered to mention simple synonyms. Many skills, jobs, companies, people, colors, etc., etc., have more than one name. We might have to deal with them in multiple languages, as well. We have many ways to represent the same date. Quantifiable things are written in different ways depending on the unit of measure, data type, number base, and so on. Our systems are usually inconsistent in handling these: they will help with such things as conversion algorithms in some cases, but not in others.

It can be very difficult to model, in a record-based system, the knowledge that different representations in different records might refer to a single underlying entity (cf. [Stamper 77], [Hall 76], [Falkenberg 76b], [Kent 77a]).

Perhaps the most blatant illustration of this is our inability to manage mailing lists. I don't know how to explain to my non-technical friends why sophisticated modern computers can't eliminate the duplications in a mailing list. The most trivial variation in the way a person writes, abbreviates, or punctuates his name or address is enough to confuse the system, and prevent it from recognizing references to the same person.

> *You would think that Kent's point about getting the data right for a mailing list would have been solved over these past forty years—but not so! I have a rather*

strange hobby of collecting examples of bizarre data situations that indicate an issue with information and how it has been modeled. Below is an actual letter I received in the mail recently. The address is correct, but look who it is addressed to? "Fname Lname"! And it is an "Exclusive Invitation" for me!

STRUCTURED NAMES

Additional confusion arises when the synonyms of an entity exhibit different kinds of structure. A person's name might be structured into three fields for first, middle, and last names; his other synonyms are single fields: employee number, Social Security number. A date (if you will accept that as an entity) has three fields in the traditional representation, but only one in Julian notation. (A Julian date is a single integer combining year and day of year: the last day of 1977 is 77365.) Now, every relationship involving a person or a date will have an uncertainty, not only with respect to the data items the fields might contain, but also with respect to the number of fields occurring in the record. Thus a binary relationship between people and dates (e.g., birthdates) could be represented in two, four, or six fields, depending on the representations chosen. But it is still fundamentally a binary relationship. Thus there is potentially a poor (and unstable) correspondence between the degree of a relationship and the number of fields used to represent it.

Note that this differs from an earlier situation where we had different kinds of entities. Here we have the same entities, but different names.

COMPOSITE NAMES AND THE SEMANTICS OF RELATIONSHIPS

Composite (e.g., qualified) names occurring in records tend to confuse the purpose and semantics (and degree) of the relationships being represented. This is especially noticeable when the composite names are themselves based on relationships. Consider, for example, the naming of employee's dependents by the two fields consisting of the employee identification plus the dependent's first name (as in Chapter 3).

The dependents in this illustration might occur in any number of relationships, being related, e.g., to benefits programs for which they are eligible, histories of claims and payments, employees responsible for them as counselors, other employee records because the dependents are themselves employees, etc. From an informational point of view, the employee on whom the person is dependent comprises a distinct, independent relationship. Yet, due to the naming convention, this information is gratuitously carried around in all the other relationships. For all of the other information, there is a single well-defined relationship that must be accessed to get the facts; but for this particular information, any relationship will do. (Of course, that gratuitous information would suddenly disappear if the naming convention for dependents was switched from qualified naming to Social Security numbers.)

A basic information model should be able to represent dependents as individual entities in these relationships, without dragging their related employees into every such context. If it is useful for applications to see dependents so identified in various relationships, then it is appropriate to define such derived "views" for the benefit of these applications. But the underlying information model need not confuse relationships with identification. A given relationship (e.g., between a dependent and a benefit program) exists independent of the means of identifying the dependent. That relationship should not be perturbed by problems or changes which might arise in the identification scheme.

Implicit Constraints

It's also worth noting that, because a record gets created or destroyed as a unit, it imposes an implicit constraint on the various pieces of information collected in the record. In particular, it imposes one-to-one correspondences between various sets of entities. Maintaining an employee number, department number, and salary in the same record guarantees that the set of employees which have salaries is exactly the same as the set of employees which are assigned to departments (in the absence of null values, of course). This is a hidden constraint that one might argue should be asserted explicitly in an information model.

Steve's Takeaways

- Record technology reflects our attempt to find efficient ways to process data. It does not reflect the natural structure of information. Record technology is such an ingrained habit of thought that most of us fail to see the limitations it forces on us.

- The logical data model is so valuable because it is technology-independent, and can therefore be reused as a starting point for multiple physical data models.

- Much of the meaning of a record is supplied by the mind of the user, who intuits many real world implications that "naturally" follow from the data.

- The information in a file consists mainly of field values occurring in records. Thus, there is likely to be a data item answering the question, "Who manages the Accounting Department?" The manager's name can be found in a field somewhere. However, there are many possible queries that can be asked involving Employee and Department that cannot be easily answered, or even be possible to answer.

- Many entity types for which considerable variability of attributes is likely to occur come to mind.

- Because a record gets created or destroyed as a unit, it imposes an implicit constraint on the various pieces of information collected in the record.

I have tried to describe information as it "really is" (at least, as it appears to me), and have kept tripping over fuzzy and overlapping concepts. This is precisely why system designers and engineers and mechanics often lose patience with academic approaches. They recognize, often implicitly, that the complexity and amorphousness of reality is unmanageable. There is an important difference between truth and utility. We want things that are useful—at least in this business; otherwise we'd be philosophers and artists.

> *Often the 80/20 rules applies to data modeling. That is, in 20 percent of the time we can complete 80 percent of the modeling. Avoid "analysis paralysis" on that last 20 percent. I believe it is okay to go for perfection in our designs, as long as we timebox managing the "complexity and amorphousness of reality."*

Reality and Tools

Perhaps it is inevitable that tools and theories never quite match. There are some opposite qualities inherent in them.

Theories tend to distinguish phenomena. A theory tends to be analytical, carefully identifying all the distinct elements and functions involved. Unifying explanations are abstracted, relationships and interactions are described, but the distinctness of the elements tends to be preserved.

Good tools, on the other hand, intermingle various phenomena. They get a job done (even better, they can do a variety of jobs). Their operation tends to intermix fragments of various theoretical phenomena; they embody a multitude of elementary functions simultaneously. That's what it usually takes to get a real job done. The end result is useful, and necessary, and profitable.

Theories tend toward completeness. A theory is defective if it does not account for all aspects of a phenomenon or function.

Tools tend to be incomplete in this respect. They incorporate those elements of a function that are useful and profitable; why bother with the rest? The justification for a tool is economic: the cost of its production and maintenance vs. the value of its problem-solving functions. This has nothing to do with completeness. (In 1975, a government official asked to have his job abolished, because nobody actually needed the services of his office. His job did have a well-defined function, in theory. "Completeness" would have dictated that his job be retained.)

Useful tools have well-defined parts, and predictable behavior. They lend themselves to solving problems we consider important, by any means we can contrive. We often solve a problem using a tool that wasn't designed for it. Tools are available to be used, don't cost too much, don't work too slowly, don't break too often, don't need too much maintenance, don't need too much training in their use, don't become obsolete too fast or too often, are profitable to the toolmaker, and preferably come with some guarantee, from a reliable toolmaker. Tools don't share many of the characteristics of theories. Completeness and generality only matter to the extent that a few tools can economically solve many of the problems we care about.

Thus the truth of things may be this: Useful things get done by tools that are an amalgam of fragments of theories. Those are the kinds of tools whose production and maintenance expense can be justified. Theories are helpful to gain understanding, which may lead to the better design of better tools. This understanding is not essential; an un-analytic instinct for building good tools is just as useful, and often gets results faster.

It may be a mistake to require a tool to fit the mold of any theory. If this be so, then we'd better be aware of when we are discussing theory and when we are discussing tools.

Data models are tools. They do not contain in themselves the "true" structure of information. What really goes on when we present a data model, e.g., hierarchies, to a user? Does he say "Aha! Of course my information is hierarchically structured; I see how the model fits my data"? Of course not. He has to learn how to use it. We generally presume that this learning is required only because of the complexity of the tool. Difficulties are initially perceived as a failure to fully understand the theory; there is an expectation that perseverance will lead to a marvelous insight into how the theory fits the problem. In fact, much of his "learning" is really a struggle to contrive some way of fitting his problem to the tool: changing the way he thinks about his information, experimenting with different ways of representing it, and perhaps even abandoning some parts of his intended application because the tool won't handle it. Much of this "learning" process is really a conditioning of his perceptions, so that he learns to accept as fact those assumptions needed to make the theory work, and to ignore or reject as trivial those cases where the theory fails.

Tools are generally orthogonal to the problems they solve, in that a given tool can be applied to a variety of problems, and a given problem can be solved in different ways with different tools. Versatility is in fact a very desirable property in a tool. It is useful then also to understand separately the characteristics of a tool and the nature of the problems to which it can be applied.

Points of View

A logical model, by its very nature, needs to be durable—at least in form, if not content. Its content should be adjusted to reflect changes in the enterprise and its information needs—only. The form of the logical model—the constructs and terms in which it is expressed—should be as impervious as possible to changes in the supporting computer technology. We can postulate that the man-machine interface will continue to evolve toward man; data processing technology will move toward handling information in ways that are natural to the people who use it. It follows then that a durable logical model should be based on constructs as close as possible to the human way of perceiving information.

> *The logical data model is much more durable than the physical data model because the logical model represents information, not how information is compromised by technology. Therefore when technology changes, the physical data model may also change, yet the logical model remains intact.*

> *In addition, Kent's statements in the prior paragraph have proven to be true today: "We can postulate that the man-machine interface will continue to evolve toward man; data processing technology will move toward handling information in ways that are natural to the people who use it." Today, technology has evolved to the point where computers are very fast, software is very user-friendly, and storage space is very inexpensive. In many cases, the compromises needed on the physical data model are minimal and therefore, the logical and physical data models often look very similar; and maybe at some point in the future, they will look identical.*

There's a catch right there: the implicit assumption that there is just one "technology" by which all people perceive information, and hence which is most natural and easy for everybody to use. There probably isn't. Human brains undoubtedly function in a variety of ways. We know that some people do their thinking primarily in terms of visual images; others hear ideas being discussed in their heads; still others may have a different mode of intuiting concepts, neither visual nor aural. Analogously, some people may structure information in their heads in tabular form, others work best with analytic subdivisions leading to hierarchies, and others naturally follow paths in a network of relationships.

> *We need to consider context in many ways on our data models. In this book, we have stressed that context plays a role in scope, abstraction, terminology, and definitions. It also plays a role in readability. That is, we can tailor what we show on the model and how we show it to a particular audience. Customer may be shown as a rectangle containing the word "Customer" for one set of users, but as an illustration of a customer for another set of users.*

This may well be the root of the debates over which data model is best, most natural, easiest to learn and use, most machine-independent, etc. The camps are probably divided up according to the way their brains function—each camp advocating the model that best approximates their own brain technology.

A View of Reality

> *I do not know where we are going, but I do know this—that wherever it is, we shall lose our way.*
>
> Sagatsa
>
> *If you're confused, it just proves you've been paying attention.*
>
> G. Kent

This book projects a philosophy that life and reality are at bottom amorphous, disordered, contradictory, inconsistent, non-rational, and non-objective. Science and much of Western philosophy have in the past presented us with the illusion that things are otherwise. Rational views of the universe are idealized models that only approximate reality. The approximations are useful. The models are successful often enough in predicting the behavior of things that they provide a useful foundation for science and technology. But they are ultimately only approximations of reality, and non-unique at that.

This bothers many of us. We don't want to confront the unreality of reality. It frightens, like the shifting ground in an earthquake. We are abruptly left without reference points, without foundations, with nothing to stand on but our imaginations, our ethereal self-awareness.

So we shrug it off, shake it away as nonsense, philosophy, fantasy. What good is it? Maybe if we shut our eyes the notion will go away.

What do we know about physical entities, about ourselves?

Lewis Thomas tells us that a human being is not exactly a single discrete living thing, but more a symbiotic interaction of hordes of discrete living things inhabiting and motivating our cells. We are each an enormously divisible social structure [Thomas].

Sociobiologists are telling us that the human being is not the unit of evolution and survival. It is our genes that are motivated to survive and perpetuate themselves. Individual people are merely vehicles whose survival serves that higher purpose—sometimes! [*Time* magazine, Aug. 1, 1977]

Our precious self image is being challenged from another quarter, too. Some scientists aren't quite so sure anymore that they can clearly distinguish between the categories of "man" and "animal." "People" might not be a well-defined category! Recent experiments have demonstrated the capabilities of chimpanzees and gorillas to acquire language, concepts, symbols, abstractions—traits held by some to be the only significant hallmarks of the human species. A lawyer is prepared to argue that such animals are entitled to some of the protections accorded individuals under the law—such animals may be "legal persons." An article in *The New York Times Magazine* of June 12, 1977, observes: "If apes have access to language, can they not be expected to reason? And if they can reason, what distinction is there remaining between man and beast?... Separately, and in some instances collectively, these animals have demonstrated the ability to converse with humans for as long as 30 minutes, to combine learned words in order to describe new situations or objects, to perceive difference and sameness, to understand 'if-then' concepts, to describe their moods, to lie, to select and use words in syntactic order, to express desire, to anticipate future events, to seek signed communication with others of their species and, in one extraordinary sequence...to force the truth from a lying human.... It's a heretical question, really. I was brought up a good Catholic. Man is man and beast is beast. I don't really think that now. You can't spend four or five years with a chimp, watch it grow up, and not realize that all the going on in her head is pretty much the same as that going on in mine...."

Which brings to mind that our vision of ourselves as uniquely intelligent creatures is also threatened from quite another quarter—the one we've been dealing with all along here. What, in some people's view, is one of the objectives of artificial intelligence, if not to endow machines with an intelligence competitive with humans? Is science fiction really mistaken in its visions of humanoids and robots functioning like, or better than, human beings? How often have those visionaries been wrong before?

In the monthly magazine published by the American Museum of Natural History, we read: "Some futurists...view the current difference between human and artificial intelligence as one of degree, not of kind, and predict that the gap between humans and machines will be crossed about the year 2000" [Jastrow]. Data processing people are fond of saying that the category of employees is a subset of the category of people. How long before we have to expand that to include animals and robots? I wonder if that question will really sound as foolish to someone reading this, say, twenty or fifty years from now.

What does all this do to our sense of identity, to our egocentric view of people as entities? If we have to rebuild our world view so radically again (as, for example, Copernicus forced us to do once before), then how much faith can we have in the permanence of any world view?

Our notions of reality are overwhelmingly dominated by the accidental configurations of our physical senses. We are very parochial in our sense of scale. Bacteria and viruses and subatomic particles are not very real to most of us, nor are galaxies. We don't really know how to comprehend them. Our concept of motion is bounded by the physiology of our eyes: the continental plates don't move, but motion pictures (sequences of still pictures!) do. Most of us think of continents and islands as permanent and discrete entities—rather than as accidents of the current water level in the oceans. Are islands and mountains such different things? Have you ever had the opportunity to observe a reservoir being filled, or emptied?

And our sense of reality is quite conditioned by the very narrow frequency range to which our eyes respond. Imagine if we couldn't see the "visible" spectrum, but could see ultra-violet, or infra-red, or X-rays—or maybe sound waves! We might not have any notion of opaque objects; everything might be translucent or transparent. Things might appear to have entirely different shapes or boundaries. We might not have such a primary notion of things having sharp or fixed boundaries; the normal mode of things might be a state of flux, like the wind or clouds or currents in the ocean. Think of perceiving people in terms of the thermal gradients around their bodies, rather than gradients in the visible spectrum.

> *There is a whole world of unstructured data that technology has now allowed us to capture. Organizations are feverishly storing and attempting analysis on complex imaging, sound, and video.*

We might have no concept of day or night. Those concepts are only so "real" and "fundamental" because we are so dependent on visible light. Clumps of heat might look like "things" to us, just as clouds do now. We might see sounds as physical things moving through the air, and we might see the wind.

Or suppose that senses other than sight dominated our world view. The universe of many animals—their sense of what things exist, and what they are—is based on smell. To them, the existence and nature of a thing is defined primarily by what it smells like. What it looks like is an occasional, trivial consideration (like the smell of things is to us). In a heavy fog, we suddenly live in a universe of things heard, rather than things seen.

The shark seems to have sense organs responding directly to electrical phenomena. What image of reality could it have, which we don't even know how to imagine? (And what view of reality do we have, which a blind person doesn't even know how to imagine? Can you even begin to imagine how it feels to have no comprehension at all of what the verb "see" means?)

To a greater or lesser extent, we all operate with somewhat different foundations for our perceptions of reality. Biologist Robert Trivers comments: "The conventional view that natural selection favors nervous systems that produce ever more accurate images of the world must be a very naïve view of mental evolution." [*Time* magazine, Aug. 1, 1977.] Among many of us, the differences are trivial. Between some of us they are enormous.

Compare your view of reality with that of a mathematical physicist, or an astronomer. (If you are one, how does it feel to be singled out as having a peculiar view?) The worldview of such people includes as regular features such notions as Einsteinian time and space, particles of light, light being bent by gravity, everything accelerating away from everything else, black holes, and seeing things (stars) that may have vanished thousands or millions of years ago. How often do these crop up in your worldview?

Your brain may be obliged to confess such views are real, but your intuition isn't. What shall we make of it? The earth does look flat, after all, doesn't it? And, no matter how much schooling we've had, we can't seem to stop thinking of the sun as rising and setting. Incidentally, do your children share your world view of this phenomenon?

"Consider how the world appears to any man, however wise and experienced in human life, who has never heard one word of what science has discovered about the Cosmos. To him the earth is flat; the sun and moon are shining objects of small size that pop up daily above an eastern rim, move through the upper air, and sink below a western edge; obviously they spend the night somewhere underground. The sky is an inverted bowl made of some blue material. The stars, tiny and rather near objects, seem as if they might be alive, for they 'come out' from the sky at evening like rabbits or rattlesnakes from their burrows, and slip back again at dawn. 'Solar system' has no meaning to him, and the concept of a 'law of gravitation' is quite unintelligible—nay, even nonsensical. For him bodies do not fall because of a law of gravitation, but rather 'because there is nothing to hold them up'—i.e., because he cannot imagine their doing anything else. He cannot conceive space without an 'up' and 'down' or even without an 'east' and 'west' in it. For him the blood does not circulate; nor does the heart pump blood; he thinks it is a place where love, kindness, and thoughts are kept. Cooling is not a removal of heat but an addition of 'cold'; leaves are not green from the chemical substance chlorophyll in them, but from the 'greenness' in them. It will be impossible to reason him out of these beliefs. He will assert them as plain, hard-headed common sense; which means that they satisfy him because they are completely adequate as a system of communication between him and his fellow men. That is, they are adequate linguistically to his social needs, and will remain so until an additional group of needs is felt and is worked out in language" [Whorf].

So far I've dealt with variations in perceived reality that I can at least describe. They are close enough to my worldview (and yours, I hope) that I can describe the differences in terms of familiar concepts. But I must acknowledge the existence of worldviews so alien to mine that I can't even grasp the central concepts. These are exemplified by some of the Eastern philosophies, various theologies, mystical cults. The Hopi Indians have a worldview of time and causality that can hardly even be expressed in our vocabulary of concepts. "I find it gratuitous to assume that a Hopi who knows only the Hopi language and the cultural ideas of his own society has the same notions, often supposed to be intuitions, of time and space that we have, and that are generally assumed to be universal. In particular, he has no general notion or intuition of time as a smooth flowing continuum in which everything in the universe proceeds at an equal rate, out of a future, through a present, into a past.... The Hopi language and culture conceals a metaphysics, such as our so-called naïve view of space and time does, or as the relativity theory does; yet it is a different metaphysics from either. In order to describe the structure of the universe according to the Hopi, it is necessary to attempt—insofar as it is possible—to make explicit this metaphysics, properly describable only in the Hopi language, by means of an approximation expressed in our own language, somewhat inadequately it is true..." [Whorf].

Do you and I have the "real" notion of time? What shall we make of contemporary physics, which wants us to believe that time passes at different rates for objects traveling at different speeds? The astronaut who has been traveling a year close to the speed of light has been gone from us for ten years? Or is it vice versa?

Language has an enormous influence on our perception of reality. Not only does it affect how we think and what we think about, but also how we perceive things in the first place. Rather than serving merely as a passive vehicle for containing our thoughts, language has an active influence on the shape of our thoughts. "...[L]anguage produces an organization of experience...language first of all is a classification and arrangement of the stream of sensory experience that results in a certain world order..." [Whorf].

Whorf quoting Edward Sapir: "Human beings do not live in the objective world alone, nor alone in the world of social activity as ordinarily understood, but are very much at the mercy of the particular language that has become the medium of expression for their society. It is quite an illusion to imagine that one adjusts to reality without the use of language and that language is merely an incidental means of solving specific problems of communication or reflection. The fact of the matter is that the 'real world' is to a large extent unconsciously built up on the language habits of the group.... We see and hear and otherwise experience very largely as we do because the language habits of our community predispose certain choices of interpretation."

"Hopi has one noun that covers every thing or being that flies, with the exception of birds, which class is denoted by another noun.... The Hopi actually call insect, airplane, and aviator all by the same word, and feel no difficulty about it.... This class seems to us too large and inclusive, but so would our class 'snow' to an Eskimo. We have the same word for falling snow, snow on the ground, snow packed hard like ice, slushy snow, wind-driven flying snow—whatever the situation may be. To an Eskimo, this all-inclusive word would be almost unthinkable; he would say that falling snow, slushy snow, and so on, are sensuously and operationally different, different things to contend with; he uses different words for them and for other kinds of snow. The Aztecs go even farther than we in the opposite direction, with 'cold,' 'ice,' and 'snow' all represented by the same basic word with different terminations; 'ice' is the noun form; 'cold,' the adjectival form; and for 'snow,' 'ice mist'" [Whorf].

We are more ready to perceive things as entities when our language happens to have nouns for them. For what reason does our language happen to have the noun "schedule" for the connection between, say, a train and a time, but no such familiar noun for the connection between a person and his salary?

The way we bundle relationships is similarly affected. If we think of the relationships "has color" and "has weight," we might be inclined to lump them into a single "has" relationship, with several kinds of entities in the second domain. But if we happen to employ the word "weighs," then that makes it easier to think of the second relationship as being distinct in its own right. By what accident of linguistic evolution do we fail to have a similar verb for the color phenomenon? ("Appears" might be a close approximation.)

Other examples: "has salary" vs. "earns," "has height" vs. what?

The accidents of vocabulary: we are most prepared to identify as entities or relationships those things for which our vocabulary happens to contain a word. The presence of such a word focuses our thinking onto what then appears as a singular phenomenon. The absence of such a word renders the thought diffuse, non-specific, non-singular.

This is all very unsatisfying. It is consistent with this philosophy of reality (perhaps even necessary, rather than just consistent) that I cannot see it applied consistently. I must accept paradoxes embedded right in the process of embracing such views. I am not, after all, such an alien creature. I see the world in much the same terms as you do. I have a name, and an employer, and a Social Security number, and a salary, and a birth date, etc., etc. There is a reasonably accurate description of me and my environment in several files. I have a wife, and children, and a car, all of which I believe to be very real. In short, I can share with you a very traditional view of reality; most of the useful activities of my daily life are predicated on such familiar foundations.

Well then, what's going on? What are these contradictions all about?

I'm really not sure, but perhaps I can try to frame an answer in terms of purpose and scope. I am convinced, at bottom, that no two people have a perception of reality that is identical in every detail. In fact, a given person has different views at different times—either trivially, because detailed facts change, or in a larger sense, such as the duality of my own views.

But there is considerable overlap in all of these views. Given the right set of people, the differences in their views may become negligible. Reducing the number of people involved greatly enhances this likelihood. This is what I mean by "scope": the number of people whose views have to be reconciled.

In addition, there is a question of purpose. Views can be reconciled with different degrees of success to serve different purposes. By reconciliation I mean a state in which the parties involved have negligible differences in that portion of their worldviews that is relevant to the purpose at hand. If an involved party holds multiple viewpoints, he may agree to use a particular one to serve the purpose at hand. Or he may be persuaded to modify his view, to serve that purpose.

If the purpose is to arrive at an absolute definition of truth and beauty, the chances of reconciliation are nil. But for the purposes of survival and the conduct of our daily lives (relatively narrow purposes), chances of reconciliation are necessarily high. I can buy food from the grocer, and ask a policeman to chase a burglar, without sharing these people's views of truth and beauty. It is an inevitable outcome of natural selection that those of us who have survived share, within a sufficiently localized community, a common view of certain basic staples of life. This is fundamental to any kind of social interaction.

If the purpose is to maintain the inventory records for a warehouse, the chances of reconciliation are again high. (How high? High enough to make the system workably acceptable to certain decision makers in management.) If the purpose is to consistently maintain the personnel, production, planning, sales, and customer data for a multi-national corporation, the chances of reconciliation are somewhat less: the purposes are broader, and there are more people's views involved.

So, at bottom, we come to this duality. In an absolute sense, there is no singular objective reality. But we can share a common enough view of it for most of our working purposes, so that reality does appear to be objective and stable.

But the chances of achieving such a shared view become poorer when we try to encompass broader purposes, and to involve more people. This is precisely why the question is becoming more relevant today: the thrust of technology is to foster interaction among greater numbers of people, and to integrate processes into monoliths serving wider and wider purposes. It is in this environment that discrepancies in fundamental assumptions will become increasingly exposed.

Steve's Takeaways

- We want things that are useful, at least in this business; otherwise, we'd be philosophers and artists. Therefore, apply the 80/20 rule to data modeling.

- Theories tend to distinguish phenomena. Good tools, on the other hand, intermingle phenomena. Theories tend toward completeness. Completeness and generality only matter to the extent that a few tools can economically solve many of the problems we care about.

- Data models are tools. They do not contain the "true" structure of information.

- Tools are generally orthogonal to the problems they solve, in that a given tool can be applied to a variety of problems, and a given problem can be solved in different ways with different tools.

- The logical data model is much more durable than the physical data model because the logical model represents information, not how information is compromised by technology.

- We need to consider context not just with scope, abstraction, terminology, and definitions, but also with readability.

- Rational views of the universe are idealized models that only approximate reality.

- Language has an enormous influence on our perception of reality.

- There is no singular objective reality. But we can share a common enough view of it for most of our working purposes, so that reality does appear to be objective and stable.

[Abrial] J.R. Abrial, "Data Semantics," in [Klimbie].

[Adams] D. Adams, *The Hitchhiker's Guide to the Galaxy*, Random House, 1979.

[ANSI 75] ANSI/X3/SPARC, Study Group on Database Management Systems, Interim Report, Feb. 1975.

[ANSI 77] *The ANSI/X3/SPARC DBMS Framework, Report of the Study Group on Database Management Systems,* (D. Tsichritzis and A. Klug, editors), AFIPS Press, 1977.

[Armstrong] W.W. Armstrong, "Dependency Structures of Database Relationships," in J.L. Rosenfeld (ed.), *Information Processing* 74, North Holland, 1974.

[Ash] W.L. Ash and E.H. Sibley, "TRAMP: An Interpretive Associative Processor With Deductive Capabilities," Proc. 1968 ACM Nat. Conf., 144-156.

[Astrahan 75] M.M. Astrahan and D.D. Chamberlin, "Implementation of a Structured English Query Language," Comm. ACM 18 (10), Oct. 1975.

[Astrahan 76] M.M. Astrahan et al., "System R: Relational Approach to Database Management," ACM Transactions on Database Systems 1 (2), June 1976, pp. 97-137.

[Bachman 75] C.W. Bachman, "Trends in Database Management—1975," National Computer Conference, 1975.

[Bachman 77] C.W. Bachman and M. Daya, "The Role Concept in Data Models," in [VLDB 77].

[Bell] A. Bell and M.R. Quillian, "Capturing Concepts in a Semantic Net," Proc. Symp. on Associative Information Techniques, Sept. 30-Oct. 1, 1968, Warren, Mich.

[Berild] S. Berild and S. Nachmens, "Some Practical Applications of CS4—A DBMS for Associative Databases," in [Nijssen 77].

[Bernstein 75] P.A. Bernstein, J.R. Swenson, and D.C. Tsichritzis, "A Unified Approach to Functional Dependencies and Relations," in [SIGMOD 75].

[Bernstein 76] P.A. Bernstein, "Synthesizing Third Normal Form Relations From Functional Dependencies," ACM Transactions on Database Systems 1 (4), Dec. 1976.

[Biller 76] H. Biller and E.J. Neuhold, "Semantics of Databases: The Semantics of Data Models," Technical Report 03/76, Institut fur Informatik, University of Stuttgart, Germany.

[Biller 77] H. Biller and E.J. Neuhold, "Concepts for the Conceptual Schema," in [Nijssen 77].

[Bobrow] D.G. Bobrow and A. Collins (ed.), *Representation and Understanding,* Academic Press, 1975.

[Boyce] R.F. Boyce and D.D. Chamberlin, "Using a Structured English Query Language as a Data Definition Facility," IBM Research Report RJ1318, Dec. 1973.

[Bracchi] G. Bracchi, P. Paolini and G. Pelagatti, "Binary Logical Associations in Data Modelling," in [Nijssen 76].

[C&A 70] "The Empty Column," Computers and Automation, Jan. 1970.

[Celko] J. Celko, *Joe Celko's Data Measurements, and Standards in SQL*, Morgan Kaufmann, 2010.

[Chamberlin 74] D.D. Chamberlin and R.F. Boyce, "SEQUEL: A Structured English Query Language," in [SIGMOD 74].

[Chamberlin 76a] D.D. Chamberlin, "Relational Database Management Systems," ACM Computing Surveys 8 (1), March 1976, pp. 43-66.

[Chamberlin 76b] D.D. Chamberlin et al., "SEQUEL 2: A Unified Approach to Data Definition, Manipulation, and Control," IBM Journal of Research and Development 20 (6), Nov. 1976, pp. 560-575.

[Chen] P.P.S. Chen, "The Entity-Relationship Model: Toward a Unified View of Data," ACM Transactions on Database Systems 1 (1), March 1976, pp. 9-36.

[Childs] D.L. Childs, "Extended Set Theory," in [VLDB 77].

[CODASYL 71] CODASYL Database Task Group Report, ACM, New York, April 1971.

[CODASYL 73] CODASYL DDL, Journal of Development, June 1973 (Supt. of Docs., U.S. Govt. Printing Office, Washington D.C., catalog no. C13.6/2:113).

[Codd 70] E.F. Codd, "A Relational Model of Data for Large Shared Data Banks," Comm. ACM 13 (6), June 1970.

[Codd 71a] E.F. Codd, "A Database Sublanguage Founded on the Relational Calculus," in [SIGFIDET 71].

[Codd 71b] E.F. Codd, "Normalized Database Structure: A Brief Tutorial," in [SIGFIDET 71].

[Codd 72] E.F. Codd, "Further Normalization of the Database Relational Model," in R. Rustin (ed.), *Database Systems (Courant Computer Science Symposia 6)*, Prentice-Hall, 1972.

[Codd 74] E.F. Codd and C.J. Date, "Interactive Support for Non-Programmers: The Relational and Network Approaches," in [SIGMOD 74-2].

[Date 74] C.J. Date and E.F. Codd, "The Relational and Network Approaches: Comparison of the Application Programming Interface," in [SIGMOD 74-2].

[Date 77] C.J. Date, *An Introduction to Database Systems (second edition)*, Addison-Wesley, 1977.

[Davies] C.T. Davies, "A Logical Concept for the Control and Management of Data," Report AR-0803-00, IBM, 1967.

[DBTG] Same as [CODASYL].

[Delobel] C. Delobel and R.G. Casey, "Decomposition of a Database and the Theory of Boolean Switching Functions," IBM Journal of Research and Development, 17 (5), Sept. 1973, pp. 374-386.

[Douque] B.C.M. Douque and G.M. Nijssen (eds.), *Database Description,* North Holland, 1975. (Proc. IFIP TC-2 Special Working Conf., Wepion, Belgium, Jan. 13-17, 1975.)

[Durchholz] R. Durchholz, "Types and Related Concepts," in [ICS 77].

[Earnest] C. Earnest, "Selection and Higher Level Structures in Networks," in [Douque].

[Engles 70] R.W. Engles, "A Tutorial on Database Organization," Annual Review in Automatic Programming, 7 (1), Pergamon Press, Oxford, 1972, pp. 1-64.

[Engles 71] R.W. Engles, "An Analysis of the April 1971 DBTG Report," in [SIGFIDET 71].

[Eswaran] K.P. Eswaran and D.D. Chamberlin, "Functional Specifications of a Subsystem for Database Integrity," in [VLDB 75], pp. 48-68.

[Fabun] Don Fabun, "Communications: The Transfer of Meaning," Glencoe Press, 1968.

[Fadous] R. Fadous and J. Forsyth, "Finding Candidate Keys for Relational Databases," in [SIGMOD 75].

[Fagin] R. Fagin, "Multivalued Dependencies and a New Normal Form for Relational Databases," ACM Transactions on Database Systems 2 (3), Sept. 1977.

[Falkenberg 76a] E. Falkenberg, "Concepts for Modelling Information," in [Nijssen 76].

[Falkenberg 76b] E. Falkenberg, "Significations: The Key To Unify Database Management," Information Systems 2 (1), 1976, pp. 19-28.

[Falkenberg 77] E. Falkenberg, "Concepts for the Coexistence Approach to Database Management," in [ICS 77].

[Folinus] J.J. Folinus, S.E. Madnick, and H.B. Schutzman, "Virtual Information in Database Systems," FDT (SIGFIDET Bulletin) 6(2) 1974.

[Furtado] A.L. Furtado, "Formal Aspects of the Relational Model," Monographs in Computer Science and Computer Applications, No. 6/76, Catholic University, Rio de Janeiro, Brazil, April 1976.

[Goguen] J.A. Goguen, "On Fuzzy Robot Planning," in [Zadeh].

[Griffith 73] R.L. Griffith and V.G. Hargan, "Theory of Idea Structures," IBM Technical Report TR02.559, April 1973.

[Griffith 75] R.L. Griffith, "Information Structures," IBM Technical Report TR03.013, May 1976.

[GUIDE-SHARE] "Database Management System Requirements," Joint Guide-Share Database Requirements Group, Nov. 1970.

[Hall 75] P.A.V. Hall, P. Hitchcock, and S.J.P. Todd, "An Algebra of Relations for Machine Computation," Second ACM Symposium on Principles of Programming Languages, Palo Alto, California, Jan. 1975.

[Hall 76] P.A.V. Hall, J. Owlett and S.J.P. Todd, "Relations and Entities," in [Nijssen 76].

[Hammer] M.M. Hammer and D.J. McLeod, "Semantic Integrity in a Relational Database System," in [VLDB 75].

[Hayakawa] S.I. Hayakawa, *Language in Thought and Action,* third edition, Harcourt Brace Jovanovich, 1972.

[Heidorn] G.E. Heidorn, "Natural Language Inputs to a Simulation Programming System," Report NPS-55HD72101A, Naval Postgraduate School, Monterey, 1972.

[Hoberman] S. Hoberman, *Data Modeling Made Simple, 2nd Edition*, Technics Publications, 2009.

[ICS 77] *International Computing Symposium 1977,* North Holland, 1975, E. Morlet and D. Ribbens (eds.). (Proc. ICS77, Liege, Belgium, April 4-7, 1977.)

[IMS] IMS/VS General Information Manual, IBM Form No. GH20-1260.

[Jardine] D.A. Jardine, *The ANSI/SPARC DBMS Model,* North Holland, 1977. (Proc. SHARE Working Conference on DBMS, Montreal, Canada, Apr. 26-30, 1976.)

[Jastrow] Robert Jastrow, "Post-Human Intelligence," Natural History 86(6), June-July 1977, pp. 12-18.

[Kent 73] W. Kent, "A Primer of Normal Forms," Technical Report TR02.600, IBM, San Jose, California, Dec. 1973.

[Kent 76] W. Kent, "New Criteria for the Conceptual Model," in [Lockemann].

[Kent 77a] W. Kent, "Entities and Relationships in Information," in [Nijssen 77].

[Kent 77b] W. Kent, "Limitations of Record Oriented Information Models," IBM Technical Report TR03.028, May 1977.

[Kerschberg 76a] L. Kerschberg, A. Klug, and D. Tsichritzis, "A Taxonomy of Data Models," in [Lockemann].

[Kerschberg 76b] L. Kerschberg, E.A. Ozkarahan, and J.E.S. Pacheco, "A Synthetic English Query Language for a Relational Associative Processor," Proc. 2nd Intl. Conf. on Software Engineering, San Francisco, 1976.

[Klimbie] J.W. Klimbie and K.L. Koffeman (eds.), *Database Management,* North Holland, 1974. (Proc. IFIP Working Conf. on Database Management, Cargese, Corsica, France, April 1-5, 1974.)

[Levien] R.E. Levien and M.E. Maron, "A Computer System for Inference Execution and Data Retrieval," Comm. ACM 1967, 10, 715-721.

[Lockemann] P.C. Lockemann and E.J. Neuhold (eds.), *Systems for Large Databases,* North Holland, 1977. (Proc. Second International Conference on Very Large Databases, Sept. 8-10, 1976, Brussels.)

[Martin] J. Martin, *Computer Data-Base Organization,* Prentice-Hall, 1975.

[McLeod] D.J. McLeod, "High Level Domain Definition in a Relational Database System," Proceedings of Conference on Data: Abstraction, Definition, and Structure, (Salt Lake City, Utah, March 22-24, 1976), ACM 1976.

[Mealy] G.H. Mealy, "Another Look at Data," Proc. AFIPS 1967 Fall Joint Computer Conf., Vol. 31.

[Meltzer 75] H.S. Meltzer, "An Overview of the Administration of Databases," Second USA-Japan Computer Conference, Tokyo, Aug. 28, 1975, pp. 365-370.

[Metaxides] A. Metaxides, discussion on p. 181 of [Douque].

[Mumford] E. Mumford and H. Sackman (eds.), *Human Choice and Computers,* North Holland, 1975.

[Nijssen 75] G.M. Nijssen, "Two Major Flaws in the CODASYL DDL 1973 and Proposed Corrections," Information Systems, Vol. 1, 1975, pp. 115-132.

[Nijssen 76] G.M. Nijssen, *Modelling in Database Management Systems,* North Holland, 1976. (Proc. IFIP TC-2 Working Conf., Freudenstadt, W. Germany, Jan. 5-9, 1976.)

[Nijssen 77] G.M. Nijssen, *Architecture and Models in Database Management Systems,* North Holland, 1977. (Proc. IFIP TC-2 Working Conf., Nice, France, Jan. 3-7, 1977.)

[Pirotte] A. Pirotte, "The Entity-Association Model: An Information-Oriented Database Model," in [ICS 77].

[Potts 08] C. Potts, *fruITion: Creating the Ultimate Corporate Strategy for Information Technology*, Technics Publications, 2008.

[Rissanen 73] J. Rissanen and C. Delobel, "Decomposition of Files, a Basis For Data Storage and Retrieval," IBM Research Report RJ1220, May 1973.

[Rissanen 77] J. Rissanen, "Independent Components of Relations," ACM Transactions on Database Systems 2 (4), Dec. 1977.

[Robinson] K.A. Robinson, "Database—The Ideas Behind the Ideas," Computer Journal 18 (1), Feb. 1975, pp. 7-11.

[Roussopoulos] N. Roussopoulos and J. Mylopoulus, "Using Semantic Networks for Database Management," in [VLDB 75], pp. 144-172.

[Sapir] E. Sapir, "Conceptual Categories in Primitive Languages," Science (74), 1931, p. 578.

[Schank] R.C. Schank and K.M. Colby, *Computer Models of Thought and Language,* W.H. Freeman, 1973.

[Schmid 75] H.A. Schmid and J.R. Swenson, "On the Semantics of the Relational Model," in [SIGMOD 75], pp. 211-223.

[Schmid 77] H.A. Schmid, "An Analysis of Some Constructs for Conceptual Models," in [Nijssen 77].

[Senko 73] M.E. Senko, E.B. Altman, M.M. Astrahan, and P.L. Fehder, "Data Structures and Accessing in Database Systems," IBM Systems J. 1973, 12, 30-93.

[Senko 75a] M.E. Senko, "The DDL in the Context of a Multilevel Structured Description: DIAM II with FORAL," in [Douque], 239-257.

[Senko 75b] M.E. Senko, "Information Systems: Records, Relations, Sets, Entities, and Things," Information Systems 1 (1), 1975, pp. 1-13.

[Senko 76] M.E. Senko, "DIAM as a Detailed Example of the ANSI SPARC Architecture," in [Nijssen 76].

[Senko 77a] M.E. Senko, "Data structures and data accessing in database systems past, present, future," IBM Systems Journal 16 (3), 1977, pp. 208-257.

[Senko 77b] M.E. Senko, "Conceptual schemas, abstract data structures, enterprise descriptions," in [ICS 77].

[Shapiro] S.C. Shapiro, "The Mind System. A Data Structure for Semantic Information Processing," Rand Corp., Santa Monica, California, Aug. 1971.

[Sharman 75] G.C.H. Sharman, "A New Model of Relational Database and High Level Languages," Technical Report TR.12.136, IBM United Kingdom, Feb. 1975.

[Sharman 77] G.C.H. Sharman, "Update-by-Dialogue: An Interactive Approach to Database Modification," in [SIGMOD 77].

[Sibley] E.H. Sibley and L. Kerschberg, "Data Architecture and Data Model Considerations," National Computer Conference, 1977.

[SIGFIDET 71] ACM SIGFIDET Workshop on Data Description, Access, and Control, Nov. 11-12, 1971, San Diego, California, E.F. Codd & A.L. Dean (eds.).

[SIGMOD 74] ACM SIGMOD Workshop on Data Description, Access, and Control, May 1-3, 1974, Ann Arbor, Mich., R. Rustin (ed.).

[SIGMOD 74-2] Volume 2 of [SIGMOD 74]: "Data Models: Data Structure Set Versus Relational".

[SIGMOD 75] ACM SIGMOD International Conference on Management of Data, May 14-16, 1975, San Jose, California, W.F. King (ed.).

[SIGMOD 77] ACM SIGMOD International Conference on Management of Data, Aug. 3-5, 1977, Toronto, Canada, D.C.P. Smith (ed.).

[Simsion 2007] G. Simsion, *Data Modeling Theory and Practice*, Technics Publications, LLC, 2007.

[Smith 77a] J.M. Smith and D.C.P. Smith, "Database Abstractions: Aggregation," Comm. ACM 20 (6), June 1977.

[Smith 77b] J.M. Smith and D.C.P. Smith, "Database Abstractions: Aggregation and Generalization," ACM Transactions on Database Systems 2 (2), June 1977.

[Smith 77c] J.M. Smith and D.C.P. Smith, "Integrated Specifications for Abstract Systems," UUCS-77-112, University of Utah, Sept. 1977.

[Sowa 76] J.F. Sowa, "Conceptual Graphs for a Database Interface," IBM J. Res. & Dev. 20 (4), July 1976.

[Sowa] J.F. Sowa, *Conceptual Structures: Information Processing in Mind and Machine,* Addison-Wesley, forthcoming.

[Stamper 73] R. Stamper, *Information in Business and Administrative Systems,* John Wiley, 1973.

[Stamper 75] R. Stamper, "Information Science for Systems Analysis," in [Mumford].

[Stamper 77] R.K. Stamper, "Physical Objects, Human Discourse, and Formal Systems," in [Nijssen 77].

[Sundgren 74] Bo Sundgren, "Conceptual Foundation of the Infological Approach to Databases," in [Klimbie].

[Sundgren 75] Bo Sundgren, *Theory of Databases,* Petrocelli, N.Y., 1975.

[Taylor] R.W. Taylor and R.L. Frank, "CODASYL Database Management Systems," ACM Computing Surveys 8 (1), March 1976, pp. 67-104.

[Thomas] Lewis Thomas, *The Lives of a Cell,* Viking Press, N.Y., 1974.

[Titman] P.J. Titman, "An Experimental Database System Using Binary Relations," in [Klimbie].

[Tsichritzis 75a] D. Tsichritzis, "A Network Framework for Relation Implementation," in [Douque].

[Tsichritzis 75b] D. Tsichritzis, "Features of a Conceptual Schema," CSRG Technical Report No. 56, University of Toronto, July 1975.

[Tsichritzis 76] D. Tsichritzis and F.H. Lochovsky, "Hierarchical Database Management Systems," ACM Computing Surveys 8 (1), March 1976, pp. 105-124.

[Tsichritzis 77] D.C. Tsichritzis and F.H Lochovsky, *Database Management Systems,* Academic Press, 1977.

[Tully] C.J. Tully, "The Unsolved Problem—A New Look At Computer Science," Computer Bulletin 2 (2), Dec. 1974.

[VLDB 75] Proceedings of the International Conference on Very Large Databases, Sept. 22-24, 1975, Framingham, Mass. (ACM, New York).

[VLDB 76] (Same as [Lockemann]).

[VLDB 77] Proceedings of the Third International Conference on Very Large Databases, Oct. 6-8, 1977, Tokyo, Japan. Database 9 (2), Fall 1977; SIGMOD Record 9 (4), Oct. 1977.

[Weber] H. Weber, "D-Graphs: A Conceptual Model for Databases," in [ICS 77].

[Whorf] Benjamin Lee Whorf, *Language, Thought, and Reality,* MIT, 1956.

[Zadeh] L.A. Zadeh, K. Fu, K. Tanaka, and M. Shimura (eds.), *Fuzzy Sets And Their Applications to Cognitive and Decision Processes,* Academic Press, 1975.

[Zemanek 72] H. Zemanek, "Some Philosophical Aspects of Information Processing," in *The Skyline of Information Processing,* North Holland, 1972 (H. Zemanek, ed.).

[Zemanek 75] H. Zemanek, "The Human Being and the Automaton," in [Mumford].

Printed in Great Britain
by Amazon